P9-AQA-298

MOBILIZING CONGREGATIONS

MOBILIZING CONGREGATIONS

How Teams Can Motivate Members and Get Things Done

John W. Wimberly Jr.

An Alban Institute Book

ROWMAN & LITTLEFIELD
Lanham • Boulder • New York • London

Published by Rowman & Littlefield
A wholly owned subsidiary of The Rowman & Littlefield Publishing
Group, Inc.
4501 Forbes Boulevard, Suite 200, Lanham, Maryland 20706
www.rowman.com

Unit A, Whitacre Mews, 26-34 Stannary Street, London SE11 4AB

Copyright © 2015 by Rowman & Littlefield

All rights reserved. No part of this book may be reproduced in any form or
by any electronic or mechanical means, including information storage and
retrieval systems, without written permission from the publisher, except by
a reviewer who may quote passages in a review.

British Library Cataloguing in Publication Information Available

Library of Congress Cataloging-in-Publication Data

Wimberly, John W.
Mobilizing congregations : how teams can motivate members and get things done / John W.
Wimberly Jr.
pages cm
Includes bibliographical references.
ISBN 978-1-56699-774-4 (cloth : alk. paper)—ISBN 978-1-56699-736-2 (pbk. : alk.
paper)—ISBN 978-1-56699-737-9 (electronic)
1. Church management. 2. Church committees. 3. Teams in the workplace. 4. Church polity.
I. Title.
BV652.W5575 2015
253—dc23
2014043965

∞™ The paper used in this publication meets the minimum requirements
of American National Standard for Information Sciences Permanence of
Paper for Printed Library Materials, ANSI/NISO Z39.48-1992.

Printed in the United States of America

CONTENTS

INTRODUCTION

I had been having the same conversation with our part-time Christian educators at Western Presbyterian Church for years. Frustrated, even angry, each one came to me and said something like, "John, I simply cannot get anyone to teach Sunday school. I'm using most of my time recruiting rather than supporting teachers and students. Our members say they don't want to miss worship to teach, or they don't want to have to come to Western Church every week for a month while they teach because they have other things to do on some of those Sunday mornings. I have tried everything and everyone, and I just can't get enough teachers." Actually, we had tried everything except one: teams.

Western's Christian educator, Debbie McKune, and I agreed to embark on a new approach. We decided to create a team of approximately four teachers for each Sunday school class. This actually meant recruiting more, rather than fewer, teachers. However, the entire group, not one or two teachers, would be responsible for teaching the class. By spreading the responsibility across a group, we hoped and prayed that more people would say "yes" to teaching.

Debbie and I were surprised at the reaction of some of the Christian education committee members to the idea of teams. They knew the current system was not working well due to a lack of teachers. However, they didn't like the idea of teams. Their concern about teams was channeled into a fair question: "If we can't get two people to teach each class, how will we ever get four?"

"Let's see if we can," Debbie and I responded. After a couple of months of discussion during which the members, in good biblical fashion, gnashed their teeth, the committee voted to make the move to teams.

Debbie and I were surprised at the responses we received when we asked people to be part of one of the teams: "So I don't have to be there every Sunday?" "I can trade off with another team member if something comes up at the last minute?" "We use teams at work, and I enjoy them." In contrast to our prior struggles recruiting people to teach, we were able to fill the teams without twisting too many arms.

As the teams began to function, wonderful things started happening. First, Debbie's phone didn't ring almost every early Sunday morning with a frantic teacher saying, "My daughter is sick, and I can't make it this morning. Can you cover for me?" Instead, the teacher with the sick daughter called a teammate who came to the rescue. This left Debbie free to be the Christian educator, not a substitute teacher.

Second, teachers began to share important insights about their students with one another. When "Jimmy" acted out, the team called a meeting and developed a strategy to work with him and his parents. No one teacher felt responsible for Jimmy. They all felt responsible. The creative approach to caring and educating a child that developed in our new team approach led to wonderful strategies to keep Jimmy engaged in class. Jimmy's parents came to me and expressed gratitude for the way the team was caring for their son.

Third, the teams developed a sense of camaraderie. People who didn't know each other became friends and trusted each other. The bonds that developed in the Sunday school wing of the church were among the strongest in the congregation.

With the success we witnessed using teams for Christian education, Western began to use teams in many other areas of its life— ushering, caring for the facilities, providing flowers for worship, and setting up the chancel, to name a few. Members who had previously been uninvolved in anything other than attending Sunday morning worship were mobilized as team members for important tasks in ministry. Technically, I suppose the engagement of more members wasn't a miracle, but it felt miraculous to those of us who recruited members for various jobs in the congregation.

As I began to read about teams and talk with other pastors about teams, I realized that Western wasn't alone in its failure to harness the power of teams to mobilize members for ministry. While teams have been well used in some congregations, especially congregations with a more conservative theological bent, they have not been widely adopted by many congregations in what used to be known as mainline denominations.

In the field of technology, marketing people talk about "early adapters" and "late adapters." For example, early adapters are the folks who bought the first iPhone. Late adapters are the folks who are buying their first iPhone in 2014. In regard to the use of teams, most mainline congregations have been neither early nor late adapters. However, it isn't too late for us to become the "*last* adapters." Perhaps we can take some solace in Jesus's encouragement that the last shall be first.

Indeed, many of us are late to the game when it comes to teams. A wide variety of organizations have relied heavily on teams for years, even decades. Military forces, corporations (most famously, high-tech companies), nonprofits, and other organizations use teams to mobilize their workers into energetic, efficient, creative workforces to accomplish the organization's mission. In so doing, they have departed, sometimes intentionally, often unintentionally, from the top down, hierarchical management styles that still dominate in many congregations. Instead of the organization being driven from the top down, a team-oriented entity is driven from within.

This book is written both for congregations that have yet to utilize the power of teams as well as those that are already using them. For the former, this book will be a primer on why teams are effective and how teams can be utilized to mobilize members. Among the topics addressed will be common resistance points raised within congregations when teams are suggested as a way to organize the work of the church, creating and training teams, and common problems that pop up as teams become operative. For those congregations already using teams, this book will be a way to consider some of the best practices of teams and team management. The use of teams puts us on a continual learning curve. There is always something new to discover about how teams function and dysfunction.

Chapter 1 will consider why teams are often more effective than committees or other ways of organizing the work and life of a congregation. We will discuss changes in our society that make many people, especially those under the age of fifty, more willing to work in teams than other forms of work groups. We will look at biblical precedents for teams, where teams have been used success- fully, the strength of team approaches to doing work, and how teams impact pastors' roles and congregational governing bodies.

In chapter 2, we discuss some of the nuts and bolts of teamwork. How do we gather the right people together to form the team? What are the competencies and personality traits needed for a team to succeed? How do we explain to teams what work they should do without being either too vague or overly controlling? How do we teach people to work in teams without micromanaging their team- work? How do the roles of congregational leaders and managers change in a team-driven congregation? How does technology help teams to do their work more efficiently?

In chapter 3, we address how managers and leaders can help teams succeed. What role does institutional context play in helping or hindering a team? When does a leader or manager move from teaching teams how to be a team to coaching them on how to be a better team? What can compromise a team's efficiency and cohesiveness? How can church staffs function as teams? What impact do teams have on the governance of a congregation?

Chapter 4 concludes the book by exploring the idea that an entire congregation has many of the characteristics of a team. In his well-known book, *The Five Dysfunctions of a Team*, Patrick Lencioni's descriptions of the dysfunctions of a team remind me of the key dysfunctions I experience in congregations as I consult with them. [1] Lack of trust, lack of accountability, and other key dysfunctions of a team are oftentimes the very things that undermine the performance of a congregation.

Perhaps the biggest mistake congregations make regarding teams is a belief that a team can be established simply by calling a few people together and naming them a team. Nothing could be further from the truth. The business world, military forces, and nonprofits have learned that teamwork is an art form. Like all forms of art, creating teams requires knowledge, hard work, and a willingness to experiment. It is my hope and prayer that congregation leaders will read this book and realize not only the power of teams but some of the skills needed to work in and manage teams. I also hope readers will contact me and begin an ongoing conversation about the problems and possibilities they discover as they begin using teams in their home congregations.

I

TEAMS AND COMMITTEES

Different in More than Name

I have always been fascinated with the *Oxford English Dictionary* (*OED*), and it is a good place to begin our discussion of teams and committees. As an unending source of information about the origins of words, the *OED* reveals a great deal about the different functions of and differences between teams and committees. This is a good starting place because, in my teaching and consulting work, the first question I always get when it comes to teams is "Aren't you just playing games with words? Aren't teams and committees basically the same thing with different names?"

The scholars who produce the *OED* found the word "team" first appeared in Old English sources where it was used as a noun to describe several oxen yoked together. In some early usages, a team described the chain used to yoke the oxen together. By yoking oxen together, a farmer is able to create power sufficient to plow fields that otherwise cannot be cultivated. A teamster is someone who drives a yoked team of horses pulling a cart or carriage. For the purposes of this book, it is also interesting to note that early on "team" was also used as a verb. "To team" meant to yoke two oxen together for more power. As proposed in this book, to team in congregations will mean to link members together in a way that produces more power.

The word "committee" was originally used in English to describe an individual "to whom some charge, trust or function is committed."[1] Over time, the word began to be used to describe a group of people to whom a responsibility was assigned. Committee came to mean "a body (two or more) of persons appointed or elected . . . for some special business or function."[2] For our purposes, the key is the root verb "to commit." Those who work on a committee commit to the work assigned them by another person or body. As a result, when a committee is created, a hierarchy of power and responsibility is immediately established. The committee is responsible to a person or body "above it." The organizational chart comes into being!

The etymology of these two words sheds significant light on the difference between a team and a committee as they will be considered in this book. Teams are groups of people who are yoked together or yoke themselves together. Unlike yoked oxen, they are not driven by taskmasters/teamsters. Instead, they are given the needed autonomy to do a task none of them can do individually. As important, they are focused not on reporting back to the body that generated the team but rather on accomplishing the task they have accepted. As a result, they are able to plow fields in ministry that would otherwise go uncultivated.

Committees are generated by a higher authority, such as a congregation's governing council. They commit to perform some special business or function on behalf of the governing body. While both teams and committees are doing work, the work of a team is usually directed toward a limited, very specific goal. A committee's work is broader in scope. For example, a Christian education committee would look at all aspects of a congregation's educational

ministry—everything from staffing to budget to curriculum to facilities. It would be concerned about building support for Christian
education within the congregation's governing body, having a say
about professional staff hires, making sure it is represented in the
governing body, creating minutes to be used by future committees,
and having regular meetings. The committee would be as much
about the decision-making process and congregational politics as it
would be about the actual work of educating. A teaching team, on
the other hand, would be thinking only about matters directly related
to teaching its students.

I must confess, when I began teaching on this subject, I initially
grew very tired and a bit irritated by an apparent unwillingness to
acknowledge the differences between committees and teams. A
Google search on the difference between teams and committees,
producing thousands of entries on the subject, helped me understand
that the church is not the only organization currently thinking
through these definitions. Furthermore, my irritation has dissipated
as I have realized that a discussion of the differences helps highlight
the transformative power of teams. Given the church's love of arguments over definitions, any congregation wanting to move to a
team-driven model needs to be able to define the difference between
the two terms.

As this brief etymological analysis reveals, the difference between committees and teams in a congregation is rooted and re-
vealed in the historical definitions and usages of the word. The
power of a committee is derived from and maintained by the body
that creates and assigns its work. Typically, committees are mandated by a congregation or denomination's bylaws. These bylaw mandated committees tend to be representative groups. Members are
chosen to represent various interests within the congregation or
ministry area. So, for example, a Christian education committee
might consist of people from the various constituencies in the minis-

try such as teachers, parents, and students. A member of the finance committee might be assigned as a member of the Christian education committee to make sure budget issues are dealt with in a proper manner.

As a result of the representational nature of such a Christian education committee, each member gives highest priority to the interests of her or his constituency, rather than the committee's task. It isn't hard to imagine the following conversation as a Christian education committee debates whether to purchase a new curriculum:

Member 1: I know some people in the congregation, including some of the parents, don't like the current curriculum. But I'm on this committee because I'm one of the teachers, so I have to let you know that there will be a major revolt by the teachers if we purchase a new curriculum. We're very comfortable with the current one. If we purchase a new curriculum, each of the teachers will have to design new lesson plans, buy new materials (because there is no budget for materials, we contribute the cost for them out of our own pockets), and do additional background reading. This is time most of us don't have to spare.

Member 2: As the youth member of the committee, I have to say most students don't like the current curriculum. If you want to get us interested in learning, we need a new curriculum. Continue to use it and you will find it more difficult to keep us engaged in the classroom.

Member 3: I sit on this committee because I serve on the finance committee. We all need to understand that we are projecting a deficit in our current budget. Money hasn't been coming in as we anticipated. Therefore, I'd be hard-pressed to recommend a major expenditure like this. We may be spending a lot of time debating something that isn't possible financially.

This example shows how a committee structure encourages a hierarchical mindset. A group "above" the committee, the church council, has to be pleased. Groups "below," the constituencies the members represent, have to be pleased. Given these dynamics, is it any wonder that committees tend to be inherently political? Committee members are focused on congregational politics and on representing others, rather than on getting the job done. We often hear people say in committee meetings, "What would the congregation think?" rather than "How can we get this done?"

A Christian education team, whose assignment is to support those who teach the faith to the children of the congregation, might have a discussion very different from the one we observed in the committee:

Team Member 1: Our job is to educate the kids. We all know that the kids don't like this curriculum. Some of the parents are also complaining. So we have a problem we need to solve.

Team Member 2: Our team has a budget. So, given the budget, can we afford a new curriculum or will we have to ask the board for more money?

Team Member 3: If we think a new curriculum is the best way to teach our kids, and we can afford it, we will need to bring our teaching teams into this discussion. Some of them have said they don't want any curriculum changes. Therefore, we need to let them know we'll help them adjust to the new curriculum. We would probably need to have special meetings with the teaching teams to explain our rationale for the change, why we think the new curriculum is better, what kind of support we will give them as they learn to use the new materials, why the kids and parents will be happier, and so on.

Team Member 4: Just as important, we need to explain why they (the teachers) will be happier. If they can't see anything in the change for themselves, they will fight us every step of the way. We need to explain our expectations that their students will be more receptive to the materials, the materials will come with lots of online support that the current curriculum doesn't offer, and they will no longer have to deal with parents who are upset because their kids don't want to come to Sunday school.

Team Member 1: So the problem we need to solve is really one of selling the new curriculum to the teachers. Let's develop some specific strategies to that end and then get busy!

The committee and the team are confronting the same issues and the same resistance points in the congregational system, but the two groups approach them differently. In a team approach, the group focuses on identifying the problem it needs to solve, decides the best way to do its job, and then determines the most efficient and effective way to get it done. Less concerned than a committee about groups or constituencies above and below it in a hierarchy, the team moves relentlessly toward getting the work done. It has a sense of autonomous, problem-solving authority that committees do not always possess.

A team is certainly accountable in the sense that it attempts to produce a quality work product for a church governing board. But a team possesses an almost exclusive focus on getting a particular task done. Indeed, it is created with a very specific task in mind. A team's primary concern is to achieve a goal, not represent constituencies within the congregation. People are "teamed" together to accomplish specific work.

In a team, the primary interpersonal dynamics flow from issues within the team itself. The personal relationships between the members are key determinants of the team's efficacy or failure in getting its work done. A committee, in contrast, may have to deal with external issues that flow into the committee's deliberations from the constituencies they represent and the board that appointed them. So, for example, a finance committee person sitting on the education committee may have a bone to pick with the personnel committee's representative on the committee. It isn't that the two don't get along personally. They have conflict when they are representing their respective constituencies.

While committees are set up with an eye to the right constituencies being represented, a team will be created with a concern for having people with the right skill sets on the team, recruiting individuals who communicate well with each other and can manage conflict among themselves, and are given sufficient resources and creative room to accomplish their work. Teammates relate to each other and their common goal. Committee members relate to those who give them their charge and those whom they represent. High-functioning committees actually attend to many of the intrateam dynamics I have mentioned. Positive interpersonal dynamics are not at the heart of a committee's mandate or function, while they are critical to a team's performance.

One pastor told me that committee members vote, while team members align themselves with each other and their common goal. That may be a bit of an overstatement, but there is a lot of truth in it. Living in a democracy, we are inclined to believe in the power and legitimacy of the vote. However, too many of us don't pay enough attention to those who lose the vote, especially close votes. When a committee makes a decision based on a close vote, the narrow margin can haunt and even sabotage the project. The "losers" redirect their energy to obtaining a revote with a different outcome.

Teams may also vote. For the most part, however, teams attempt to reach a consensus to avoid the potential for bitterness among those who lose a vote. (While a committee can also attempt to use the consensus model, it is far more difficult to achieve a consensus when individuals are representing someone else's interests rather than their own instincts as a decision-making conversation evolves.) A team doesn't conduct a vote and disband, as do many committees. As soon as the vote is taken, teams understand that they will have to work together on the project. Decisions don't have any meaning in and of themselves. In a team setting, a decision is framed by the larger task at hand and the ongoing, interpersonal dynamics among team members. Therefore, teams know they have to work through differences in order to stay focused on their performance goals. Teams are so laser-focused on performance that their members quickly move from "What we are going to do?" to "How are we going to do it?" and "Let's do it!" Team members are trained to understand that once a team makes a decision, implementing the decision is the only thing that matters.

It is not unusual for someone to ask me, "Why doesn't a committee operate this way?" Committees are not always set up to do something themselves. They are usually set up to organize others to do something. Committees tend to be more about decision making than "doing." Once a committee has made a decision, it can say to itself, "Mission accomplished." When a team makes a decision, it says, "Mission begun."

In one interview about teams, a pastor told me, "Committees exist to say 'no.'" Again, this is an overstatement. However, it reflects the experience of many congregations. My father, also a pastor, once told me, "When our congregation's session [governing body] refers a time-sensitive proposal to a committee, I cringe. Either the committee says 'no' or, by the time the committee reports back to us, its recommendations are irrelevant, because the moment for action has passed." When a team is given a job, the team is to get it done as quickly, efficiently, and effectively as possible.

Another difference between committees and teams is in the ways that leadership manifests itself. While teams have leaders, the leadership function is shared by team members. In high-functioning teams (we will discuss this further in a later chapter), each member considers him- or herself to be a leader. As important, each team member considers every other team member to be a leader. For example, in an optimum corporate leadership team, when the team is discussing finances, the vice president for finance leads the discussion. When they are discussing personnel, the vice president for human resources leads the discussion. The chief executive officer (CEO) is the team leader. But the CEO is a leader of leaders, not a leader of subordinates.

Committees, on the other hand, have a chairperson or moderator. Shared leadership in a committee would probably mean leadership consisted of cochairs. But, generally, it does not mean that everyone on the committee is considered a committee leader. The chairperson is the acknowledged leader, often appointed by the church board that authorized the committee's work in the first place. The chairperson is normally the communication channel through whom most decisions must pass. The chairperson passes along instructions or communications from the congregation's governing board to the committee members and communicates the committee's decisions back to the board.

The differences between teams and committees can guide a congregation in deciding when to use each structure. If a congregation needs a highly representative and accountable group for a special function, then a committee is probably in order. For example, a pastoral search committee usually needs to be considered representative of the larger congregation in order for its recommendations to be respected and accepted. If the congregation needs to get a job done as efficiently and creatively as possible, then a team is probably in order. For example, if the congregation needs to engage in a capital campaign, specific fundraising and communication skill sets on a team may be more important than the group being representative.

Let's think about starting a mission program. Is the best organizational strategy to use a team or committee? If the primary mover behind the mission program start-up is a traditional mission committee, it will be subject to all the issues a committee considers: "Will we have to take away money from a current mission effort to fund this new one?" "Who will staff the new program? If it is the associate pastor, what will she eliminate in her current job description to work on the new program?" "Shouldn't we get the feedback of the session as to whether or not it is a good idea?" These are all valid questions. However, they all reflect organizational concerns.

Another way to start a new mission program is for the pastor or someone else to recognize that there is some energy around a particular, felt need in the community. The pastor was teaching an adult class, during which a number of people said that someone needs to get the congregation involved in homeless ministry. As important, several people volunteered to work on the idea.

In this model, a team will self-select. They will find each other or the pastor will lead interested people to the team. It might begin with a Sunday worship announcement in which the liturgist says, "Anyone who is interested in seeing if we can create a ministry with the homeless, please see Sally James after worship. Sally, please raise your hand so people can see where you are." A small group forms and begins to think through what it will take to get a homeless ministry going. Instead of looking at the church budget for money, they brainstorm about ways to find new funding. Not looking for church staff support, they consider how the program can be self-managing. Rather than going to the church council first, they approach them with a start-up plan once it comes together. This isn't a hypothetical situation. In 1983, Western Presbyterian Church and a group of other congregations in the Foggy Bottom neighborhood of Washington, DC, empowered a team of individuals to start Miriam's Kitchen for the Homeless. The team found the money, volunteers, and food. The homeless found them! Thirty years later, Miriam's Kitchen is an almost two-million-dollar-a-year program.

Of course, one might argue, a third option would have been to start the program with a representative team. However, as we have been discussing, the qualifications for team members have little to do with representing various constituencies in a congregation. They have to do with skills and the ability to work with others. If a team is representative, but members do not possess the skills and personalities needed to get the job done, the team will fail.

Another way to define the specific role of teams is found in an excellent book, *Governance and Ministry: Rethinking Board Leadership*, by congregational consultant Dan Hotchkiss. In the book, Hotchkiss distinguishes between two spheres of leadership in a congregation—governance and ministry. At first, I balked at the distinction, because I think governance is an important form of ministry in and of itself. However, Hotchkiss's distinction helpfully illuminates the way congregations manage and mismanage their work. To Hotchkiss,

> [g]overnance includes the top-level tasks of articulating the mission, selecting a strategy for getting there, making sure it happens, and ensuring that people and property are protected against harm. Ministry is everything else: the daily, practical work of the congregation, including the rest of the decisions that must be made about what to do and how.[3]

Hotchkiss contends that much of what is called governance may require some committees to be established by the church governing board while much of what is called ministry may best be accomplished through the use of teams. He cites the following as committees that might typically be created: finance, personnel, or nursery school.

As envisioned by Hotchkiss, committees exist to do work assigned by the congregation's governing board, and the work of committees fulfills responsibilities assigned by the congregation's bylaws to the governing board. "Committees write reports, make recommendations and gather information. Teams, on the other hand, produce practical results."[4]

Hotchkiss's differentiation between committees and teams is consistent with the origins of the words "team" and "committee." A committee is in a constant relationship with the governing body that creates it. A team is focused not on governance relationships but on a work product—a Christian education class, a mission program, or a well-organized worship space.

WHY TEAMS?

From my experience and research, I have come to the conclusion that committees should no longer serve as the default option for accomplishing the work of the church. Yes, some congregations will need to have certain nominating and other constitutionally mandated committees. However, much of a congregation's work can and should be done in teams because, frankly, teams are more effective.

Western Presbyterian Church in Washington, DC, the urban congregation where I served from 1983 to 2012, morphed from a small core of about seventy members, most of them over the age of seventy, to a 350-member congregation filled with people under the age of forty-five. By 2000, more than one-half of our members were under the age of forty-five. A decade later, the percentage of under-forty-five members had increased to approximately 66 percent. Of all the changes that took place as our congregation went through this transformation, one of the most important was the movement from committees to teams. When I asked people under forty-five to serve on a committee, they almost instinctively said "no." To them, committees meant attending meetings every month, whether meetings were needed or not; reading and approving committee minutes, agendas, and budgets; serving for specific terms; and, God forbid, the possibility that he or she might end up as committee chair. Unfortunately, these stereotypes are rooted in the reality of congregational committee life. As a result, younger members routinely replied to my request to serve on a committee, "I'll be glad to help, but I just don't want to serve on a committee." Older individuals, in contrast, might complain about serving on a committee but seemed to accept it as a "cost of discipleship."

In contrast, I noticed that if I asked younger members to serve on a team or task force, they responded, "Well, what does the team do?" We need to pay attention to the verb "do" in that response. Research on generational preferences reveals that the younger generations clearly want to *do* something. They do not associate committees with doing. In their stereotype of a committee, teams "do," while committees talk or plan about "doing."

Jean Twenge is a psychology professor who has written about generational differences. As do I, she urges caution in making broad generalizations about generations because there are always large numbers of people in any generation who do not fit their particular generation's profile. Furthermore, each younger generation is met with resistance from older generations that are comfortable with their ways of doing things. Ron Perlstein, an expert on the way demographics function in political campaigns, also cautions against thinking that demographic types are absolutely predictive. He notes the way people within a specific demographic group differ from one another. As important, he contends that large segments in demographic groups can morph into something very different from the larger group's tendencies.

All of that being said, Twenge observes a strong preference for teamwork in the millennial generation (born 1982–1992). In a *New York Times* interview, she cites the work of Anne Loehr, who helps companies and organizations create multigenerational workforces. According to Twenge, Loehr says, "Many of the millennials grew up participating in family meetings and being coached for academics and sports. . . . Many were on teams at an early age, where they became accustomed to being included, having their input valued and working together as equals." Unlike millennials, baby boomers (born 1946–1964), says Twenge, are more likely to be comfortable in top-down structures, while generation X individuals (born 1964–1982) may be less team oriented than millennials and more focused on personal vocational goals.[5]

My experience with generation X in the church has been that, while they may not be overly excited about any type of group work, they definitely prefer teams to the top-down, committee model. Furthermore, I believe it is possible to meld team and individual goals to satisfy gen Xers.

When I first started in ministry in the 1970s, I heard people say that the way to work one's way up into a congregational leadership position was to serve on a committee. It was true. Committees were viewed as the minor leagues. A person could prove his or her worth in a committee and then end up on the big league of a congregation's governing board.

In contrast, teams do not foster a "work your way up" approach to life. They offer church members a "let's do it now" approach.

This has great appeal to many in the younger generations who seem to be more focused on getting a particular job done versus upward organizational leadership mobility. Some of the resistance to teams from the baby boomers may be rooted in these dynamics. Boomers have "paid their dues" in the church over the past twenty to forty years. As a result, they sit on governing boards and chair committees, possessing significant power within a congregation's governance system. Not surprisingly, some boomers enjoy their power and are reluctant to let go of it in favor of a more decentralized system of teams.

Once I noticed a tendency among younger members to welcome team assignments, we began to use teams increasingly at Western, simply because it was easier to get people to do the work. It wasn't until I read Daniel Pink's book *Drive: The Surprising Truth about What Motivates Us* that I gained more insight into why teams have gained favor in the workplace and elsewhere. In *Drive*, Pink makes a strong case that we can no longer motivate workers using the carrot-and-stick method that often worked in the past. Teams are not typically motivated by external reward systems. Instead, the rewards are internally driven. So, for example, on a team, I am more concerned about not letting down my teammates than I am about getting a bonus for succeeding. While the issue of how an organization rewards individuals who reach performance goals is not central to our discussion of teams, the issue of what motivates people is directly relevant. In the twenty-first century, teams are proving to be more effective motivators than nonteam or committee-driven groupings.

Pink directs us to three factors that motivate people: autonomy, mastery, and purpose. Top-down, command-and-control management is being displaced by management styles that encourage individuals and teams to work with autonomy to achieve set performance measures. People want to be good at their jobs. Effective managers help employees and teams master their work. The highest motivator is a clear sense of purpose. If we can link a team or individual's work to the greater ends of our faith, they will operate at extremely high levels. When twenty-first-century people are given autonomy, empowered to master their work, and linked to visionary purposes, they are highly motivated and more likely to accomplish their goals. While the effort of volunteers in a congregation isn't work per se, their efforts are the work of the church. When these dedicated congregational members experience autonomy, mastery, and purpose when performing the work of the church, they are much more likely to accomplish their own, as well as the congregation's, goals. It is my contention and experience that teams unleash these three factors in ways the traditional committee system does not.

Pink draws on the work of leaders in the field of positive psychology such as Martin Seligman and Mihaly Csikszentmihalyi. These scholars direct our attention away from dysfunction and problematic behavior and focus instead on well-being and effective functioning. Congregations would be wise to do the same. Let's stop spending so much time studying what doesn't work and begin studying what does work! Using the mindset of positive psychology to learn how to grow our congregations, we wouldn't study how to avoid all the problems of a stagnant faith community. Instead, we would study and emulate the behavior of a growing congregation. Sounds like common sense, doesn't it? It is actually totally counter to much of what we do when we analyze problems. In congregational life, we almost intuitively seek to avoid mistakes others have made, when we should be seeking to model the actions of successful clergy and congregations.

AUTONOMY

Autonomy is at the heart of how teams operate. Pink maintains that top-down management is a problem, not a solution, for those who wish to motivate people within an organization. He calls on organizations to create a "renaissance of self-direction." Pink cites a 2004 study at Cornell University in which researchers analyzed two types of businesses. One type featured a top-down, control-oriented management style, while the other management type offered workers considerable autonomy in deciding how to get their work done. Pink says, "The businesses that offered autonomy grew at four times the rate of the control-oriented firms and had one-third the turnover."[6]

To me, the retention issue rate is as important as the growth of these businesses. Companies such as General Electric have learned that developing talent from within is a far superior strategy to bringing outside talent into the company. For one thing, the outsider needs to learn the GE culture. The insider is already knowledgeable about the culture and its expectations.

In like manner, the Alban Institute and others have found that congregations retaining talented staff are far more likely to grow than those that are constantly searching for new staff to replace effective staff who have left the congregation. Continually searching for and training new staff is exhausting. In the same way, a congregation builds autonomous lay leadership when members remain in place in a particular area of ministry. As teams work together, they can develop more focused ministry skills than organizationally oriented committees where members tend to move on and off the committee as their terms of service expire.

It is my guess that much of the resistance to using teams (versus an established committee system) is rooted in an unwillingness by those with some perceived or real power over a current committee to "let go." For example, a governing council in a congregation knows how to control the behavior of committees. (Well, usually they know.) However, they don't know how to control autonomous teams, or a religious education committee chair may not trust teaching teams to function autonomously.

When I talk about teams in my management seminars, people inevitably ask, "Well, that sounds good. But who is in control?" For example, from both heads of staff and chairs of personnel committees, I hear, "Are the associate pastor and the head of staff equals on a staff team, or is the head of staff still the boss?" The short answer is both. A longer answer to this important question regarding authority will come later in the book. However, for now, it is important to recognize that moving to a team approach in the church does, in fact, mean giving the teams the autonomy they need to do their assigned task. What they need will be determined in an ongoing dialogue with the person or group to which the team is accountable.

While teams are accountable to those who create them, they have an even stronger sense of accountability to themselves. Team members feel primarily accountable to other team members. In articles about various military conflicts, we learn that when a small team of soldiers is sent into battle, they often tell reporters that they are fighting for each other, not so much for the United States itself. Shortly after major combat operations ended in Iraq on May 1, 2010, Dr. Leonard Wong from the U.S. Army War College's Strategic Studies Institute and a team of researchers went to Iraq to study why soldiers fight.

> The team went to the battlefield for the interviews because they wanted to speak with the soldiers while events were still fresh in their minds. The team asked the soldiers the same question Stouffer asked soldiers in his 1949 study—Generally, in your combat experience, what was most important to you in making you want to keep going and do as well as you did. American soldiers in Iraq responded similarly to their ancestors about

wanting to return home, but the most frequent response given for combat motivation was fighting for my buddies, Wong's report said.[7]

What do Pink and others mean by autonomy? Pink says that workers have autonomy when they possess "autonomy over the four T's: their task, their time, their technique, and their team."[8] I would like to add and start with a fifth T: trust. The mere thought of teams having such freedom can be daunting for congregational leadership such as a governing council or head of staff. However, as the demonstrated effectiveness of teams in businesses, the military forces, major nonprofits, and many growing congregations proves, it is time to overcome fears of losing control and demonstrate the spiritual quality of trust.

TRUST

Think about how much energy is spent trying to retain control of committees and staff members. Just how successful are those efforts? If your experience is anything like mine or that of many of my colleagues in ministry, your efforts are rarely successful. Trying to control the work schedule of his staff, a pastor in Washington, DC, micromanaged his secretary and janitor. His efforts at control made everyone unhappy and no one more efficient. Staff discontent was a factor in him leaving the ministry for another job. As important, while the effort to retain control occasionally succeeds, far more often it brings frustration and anger to those controlled. There has to be a better way. There is. Trust teams by giving them autonomy to do their tasks with the techniques they choose on a timeline they create.

TASK

Can we learn to trust teams to do their assigned tasks the way they think is best? Can we give them the autonomy to come up with ideas for ministry that never occurred to us? Some of the corporate world's most successful companies have employed such trust. Companies in industries as different from one another as Google and 3M have long given their employees significant time during the week to do whatever they want. That is correct: whatever they want. Such freedom generated ideas as profitable as Google's Gmail and 3M's Post-it Notes.

Paul and his quickly developed team of colleagues understood Jesus's commandment or task of spreading the Gospel to the ends of the earth in a radically new way. They wanted to take the Gospel to other parts of the world. Using their creativity, they carried out the assigned task in a way few had dared imagine possible.

TECHNIQUE

As important for Christians, Jesus gave his disciples enormous freedom as to how we might do God's will. He laid out the tasks for his disciples clearly (although not everyone got it). We are to teach, heal, work for justice, and preach the Gospel, among other tasks. However, he rarely told us exactly how we should accomplish our tasks.

To some, Jesus's lack of specificity in regard to how we are to do our work is disconcerting. As a result, the church has been arguing about how to carry out our work for two thousand years. In my lifetime, there have been arguments as to whether or not women or members of the LGBT community should be engaged in carrying out the church's work. But it is a healthy debate that leads to every generation having to figure out how to carry out the work of the church in its time and place. It is the type of debate that healthy teams have in corporations, nonprofits, and the military forces.

Part of this debate also involves workload. Do we have enough work as a team? Too little work? Is the work being carried out in a proportionate manner by each team member, or are a few teammates carrying the load for the others? Rather than having these issues dictated or even mediated by a "boss," the team approach forces team members to debate and resolve workload issues as they develop.

Jesus trusted us to do the core work of the church in the way we thought best. He felt no need to control how each of us would carry out his commandments. In so doing, he acknowledged that what was best for ministry in the first century might not necessarily be best in the twenty-first century. "Going forward, let each team figure it out faithfully and creatively," he thought to himself. When he sent his disciples out in teams of two, he told them what to take for the journey but let them devise their own team strategies to accomplish their work. Can we exhibit the same level of trust in each other today?

Giving teams the freedom to do their work in ways they deem best is crucial to truly autonomous teams. Prior to entering the ministry, I worked at the Oscar Mayer meatpacking company in Madison, Wisconsin, for a few years. From time to time, industrial engineers would appear to time and analyze our work patterns. Almost invariably, the engineers made suggestions as to how we could speed up our work, even though we were getting paid on a bonus system in which we got paid more to produce more.

The industrial engineers thought they knew better than our production teams how to do the work. Were they ever right? Of course, everybody is correct some of the time. But telling people that they are inefficient, even though they have been doing a job for years and years and, based on the bonus system, are doing their work at a rate above what the company considers 100 percent effort, is probably not going to produce good results. What was inefficient was the effort to micromanage the highly efficient work teams that made Oscar Mayer a model of profitability in a highly competitive industry. Then there is the futility factor to consider. When all was said and done, the industrial engineers did their studies, made their recommendations, and returned to their offices, and we resumed doing our jobs the way we knew was best and got us the largest bonus!

Pastors or church boards who tell their music team (usually consisting of a choir director and choir) how to do their job make the same mistake as Oscar Mayer's industrial engineers made. Over the years/decades/centuries, attempts to micromanage musicians have created incredible conflict in congregations. A better management style is to hold the music team responsible for their product—the music in worship. Tell them what the congregation wants in terms of the larger issues: themes in lyrics, styles of music, congregational participation in music, and the like. Then let the musicians create the finished product.

TIME

Autonomy regarding time is a key ingredient of any true freedom. If I go to work and someone else has total control over the way I spend my time, I have little opportunity to be creative or do the job in a manner that I feel is most effective. As bad, we are being held accountable for the use of our time without being able to shape how we use our time. If congregational managers and leaders stop focusing so much on how time is used by staff, committees, and teams and instead focus on whether or not the job gets done, we are more likely to get the results we want.

I knew a head of staff who asked his staff team to account for their time in fifteen-minute increments, much the way attorneys in large corporate law firms have to keep track of their billing hours in fifteen-minute increments. In addition to wasting a lot of time keeping track of time, this approach avoided the question the head of staff should have been asking his staff: Are you accomplishing what you were assigned to do? Effective managers are far more concerned about end products than they are on how the end product is produced. First and foremost, we need to manage results, not time. Effective organizations manage by empowering teammates to hold each other accountable regarding end results.

TEAM MEMBERSHIP

Another characteristic in Pink's description of autonomy speaks to team membership. For teams to be truly autonomous, teams must have a say about their membership. Allowing team members significant input regarding their membership means that (1) everyone who joins or remains with the team must agree with the team's internal contract regarding the work to be done, behavioral covenants, and performance measures, and (2) the team acknowledges that it has the appropriate personnel to get the task accomplished.

In some cases, teams can be self-selecting. In other instances, a team may be created by the pastor, church council, or standing committee. In either case, the members may turn out not to be the right mix. Certain skills or personality types may be missing. At that point, team membership may need to be changed, either on the initiative of the team (the best case scenario) or by congregational leadership. Later in the book, we will discuss in more detail the issues involved in creating a team.

MASTERY

In addition to the importance of autonomy in motivating today's workers, Pink rightly helps us realize that good motivators understand the difference between doing and mastering a job. As a head of staff, I did some things right. But when I read Pink's commentary on the importance of nurturing a staff member's mastery of her or his job, I realized I hadn't been doing a good enough job of helping our staff improve and master their skill sets. I expected our staff members to do their jobs well. I asked them what they needed to perform well and tried to help them get it. I did some coaching. But did I intentionally focus on helping them master their jobs? Not to the degree that Pink has convinced me is necessary.

Pink makes the point that most of us not only want to be good at our jobs; we want to get better at our work as the years pass. If we have a person on our staff who isn't interested in mastering his or her job, we get rid of the person and hire someone who is. A key to motivating today's workforce is to help them master their craft, to increase and improve their job skills. A janitor can learn to use new equipment and products; a secretary can master new aspects of complicated software; a music director can widen her or his repertoire of music. As a staff team is established, helping team members master their roles should be an explicit part of the team's function. It is also a key role for a team leader. In congregations, the leader of the staff team is usually the head of staff.

The beauty of employing mastery as a motivational tool is that 100 percent mastery of any vocational skill set can never be accomplished. The world's greatest golfer thinks she can still improve her game. A great preacher always knows that the best sermon is yet to be preached. The very pursuit of mastery has a "just beyond the horizon" aspect to it. The more we master our vocation, the more we realize how much we have yet to learn. Our desire to stretch ourselves to higher levels of performance fuels the motivation to improve our skills.

Mastery is related to the goals we embrace when we enter a profession. Most mechanics want to be known as the best mechanic in town. The same is true with clergy and congregational staff. I've never worked with a church musician who didn't think he or she was great but wanted to be greater. We want to perform in a high-quality manner time after time. Indeed, we want our performance to be increasing over time. To do so, we must learn new, and perfect existing, skills. Teams should encourage a bit of both.

In staff teams where the head of staff is seen as a member of the staff, not just as the leader, I have observed heads of staff seek out the counsel of other team members. They ask, "How can I be a better head of staff?" and "Are there things I can do better that will help you as a fellow team member?" Such heads of staff are seeking to master their job with the help and support of their team members. It is a beautiful thing to behold.

If I were still a head of staff, I would be asking my staff team (individually and as a group), "If you could become the best secretary, janitor, or music director, what would you need? Take a minute and envision yourself performing your job in a near perfect manner? What can we do as a team to help you realize that vision? What do you need in the way of resources, training, and support to get there? Do you need some time away from your regular duties to master a specific new skill? What can I do as the team leader to help you reach your vision?"

PURPOSE

Polling consistently shows that what motivates people to perform well in their jobs is not money. Polls reveal that we are inspired when our work relates to the accomplishment of a greater purpose that transcends us as individuals. Who has a higher purpose than a congregation? We have come together to praise and serve God. Beat that! As we establish teams, let us make sure we explicitly connect them to the role they play in the grander scheme of God's redemption of the world.

In my denomination, the Presbyterian Church (USA), we too often fail to articulate our purpose. We all know our purpose. It is stated clearly at the beginning of the Westminister Shorter Catechism: "Humanity's chief end is to glorify God, and to enjoy God forever."[9] It is this purpose that brought us to and keeps us in the church. But we don't employ purpose as a motivational strategy. My guess is that other denominations and congregations fail in the same way. We fail explicitly and clearly to link our work to the higher purpose to which God calls us. Why are we not framing the work of the church as done by staff, governing boards, committees, and teams in terms of our higher calling?

After reading Pink's book, I said to our secretary, "One of the goals of this congregation is to be a welcoming congregation. Jesus made all kinds of people feel valued who previously felt unvalued by the world. Welcoming people as valued children of God is at the heart of what a Christian congregation should be. We want people to feel precious, loved, and respected by God and us. Shenella, the way you greet people at the door, on the phone, and in the office is incredibly warm and welcoming. You show that we value and respect each person who enters our doors. By doing so, you are helping us realize one of our most important goals."

I told our janitor, "Gaston, we have made growing our Sunday school an important goal. We believe that God wants us to teach the next generation the truths of the Gospel. Parents today demand that their kids be in a clean, safe, attractive environment. Your work creating that environment gives those parents what they want. You are helping us realize one of the primary things we believe God wants us to do."

Over the years, I had made those comments in one way or another. But Pink helped me realize that I needed to *explicitly* link the work of all the teams in the congregation, including the staff team, to the higher purpose to which God calls us. Later in the book, we will see that a key to successful teams is starting with a clear statement of purpose. It not only helps teams function better; it motivates them.

Research and polling show purpose to be especially important to millennials. In an article in the *New York Times* on millennials, scholars Emily Esfahani Smith and Jennifer Aaker write, "Millennials appear to be more interested in living lives defined by meaning than by what some would call happiness. They report being less focused on financial success than they are on making a difference."[10] This aligns perfectly with Pink's contention that the best way to motivate younger generations is to stress the importance and purpose of their work. Say Smith and Aaker, "When individuals adopt what we call a meaning mind-set—that is, they seek connections, give to others, and orient themselves to a larger purpose—clear benefits can result, including improved psychological well-being, more creativity, and enhanced work performance. Workers who find their jobs meaningful are more engaged and less likely to leave their current positions."[11] When we create teams who have a clear purpose related to the higher goals of our congregation, younger generations will see them as opportunities to add meaning to their lives.

The analysis of motivation by Pink and many other scholars moves us beyond the vague rhetoric about "empowerment" and "enabling" that has dominated the discussion of leadership in the church for decades. In the place of such overused terms, Pink and others direct us to the specific tasks of establishing autonomous teams, helping teams master their jobs, and linking the efforts of teams firmly and clearly to the greater purposes of God as discerned by the congregation. By focusing on these three tasks, we are more likely to strike chords that resonate with the younger generations who want to serve in the church but probably don't want to serve on a committee.

Until Vatican II, the Roman Catholic Church expected its members to adjust to a foreign language (Latin) in worship. Today, we expect younger members to adapt to a foreign language called committees. Younger generations are used to operating in teams in their workplaces and other areas of their lives. The workplace is increasingly organized into teams. Corporations depend on executive management teams, communication teams, research and design teams, and facilities teams, to name a few. Many institutions of higher learning organize students into teams. In my executive MBA program at George Washington University, we were placed in teams and told that one-half of our grade would come from our team projects. Military forces rely on teams. The Osama Bin Laden saga was ended by a highly trained, closely knit team of Navy SEALs. Managers sat in an office in Washington, DC, watching and listening to the team operate in distant Pakistan. An emergency room staff is an amazing team to watch, with no hierarchy of doctors over nurses or aides. Everyone on the team has a role and plays it, because there is no time to work through a hierarchy. One of DC's premier nonprofits, Miriam's Kitchen for the Homeless, located at Western Church, uses teams to serve the homeless. It is no accident that its volunteer base is mostly under the age of forty or that there is a waiting list to volunteer at Miriam's. People want to be a part of the team.

CHANGING ROLES FOR PASTORS AND
CONGREGATIONAL GOVERNING BODIES

In chapter 3, we will deal in depth with the management and leadership of teams. However, before leaving the current discussion, I want to stress that a team-driven congregation involves leadership and management approaches that are very different from the committee-driven style used by American congregations for generations. Committee-driven congregations are designed to control what work is to be done and ensure it will be done in a particular way. Congregational leaders, including clergy, typically want to select the people who do the job, receive minutes from the committee to review its work, and feel free to intervene if they don't like the strategies employed by the committee.

In team-driven congregations, clergy and governing boards give up the quest for control in exchange for better productivity and greater satisfaction from team members. These congregational leaders are willing to evaluate teams based on the work produced rather than engage in ongoing oversight of how the work is being done. They allow teams to find their own members, organize and perform their own work, and improvise as needed.

In the Presbyterian Church, a phrase is repeated in mantra-like fashion. We say that things need to be done "decently and in order." Committees fit nicely into such a tidy worldview. In contrast, team-driven congregations simply say, "We want things done." Not every team gets its work done "decently and in order." Some teams scramble. Some teams have multiple false starts before they get going. Some teams have heated internal arguments as they get their work done. But in a team-driven congregation, the emphasis is on results, not process (decently and in order).

As we move to the next chapter's discussion about the nuts and bolts of what makes a great team, we need to put aside our control needs and focus on the joy we experience when a job is done efficiently and well. For therein lies the brilliance of a team-driven approach to congregational work.

2

STARTING TEAMS

Having considered the differences between teams and committees along with why teams are oftentimes a more effective way to mobilize the energy of a congregation's members, we will now discuss some nuts-and-bolts issues about gathering and organizing teams. Because they are commonly used in the workplace and nonprofit community organizations, it is easy to take for granted that everyone knows how to establish and maintain a team. Nothing could be further from the truth. In fact, one of the primary problems with teams can be a lack of intentionality in setting them up and managing them.

In the literature on teams, one sees a consensus on the basic work needed to establish and maintain healthy teams. In this chapter, I collate into a series of steps the various tasks required to have effective teams. The steps are simple and straightforward to describe: create, coach, and end. However, they are not so simple and straightforward to execute.

In particular, we will look at creating and coaching teams. There are three key actions we must take to create a team. First, we must generate a clear sense of the direction for a team. What is its job? Second, we need to recruit people who have the proper skills and personalities for the assigned task. Third, we need to ensure the team has the resources it needs to get its work done.

Beginning something new, like a team, is a crucial moment routinely ignored in the life of congregations. Too often, we begin a start-up without properly planning or equipping the team. We are then surprised when the project doesn't work out.

An existing congregational system will change whenever something new enters it, whether it be a new pastor, new team, or new program. Too often, we are inclined to take team members' knowledge of the system in which they exist as a given. However, for most congregational members (and even some clergy), the ways of their church's system are a mystery. Therefore, when establishing a new team, we need to educate their members about the system in which they will be working.

Corporations usually do not allow new employees to go to work without some type of program that helps them understand the company culture. Apple takes this task so seriously that they established Apple University for their employees. According to the *New York Times*, Steve Jobs created the university "as a way to inculcate employees into Apple's business culture and educate them about its history, particularly as the company grew and the tech business changed."[1] Apple considers the university such a key part of its success that its operations are a company secret. Employees are banned from talking about what they experience in the university!

As we establish teams in our churches, let us seize the chance to sit down with team members and discuss the congregational culture in which they will operate. What are the idiosyncrasies of our particular culture? Where are the landmines to be avoided? What are the strengths to be tapped? When a congregational culture is properly understood, the likelihood of a team succeeding within that unique system increases exponentially.

Of course, such a discussion assumes that congregational leadership has done a thorough job of thinking through its system. If that hasn't taken place, it should be at the top of the leadership's agenda. A good starting point for understanding congregational systems is the stellar work of Rabbi Edwin Friedman in his book *Generation to Generation*.[2] I highly recommend it.

CREATING A CLEAR SENSE OF DIRECTION

Prior to creating a team, a staff member, governing board, or committee needs to determine its purpose. Organizations, in general, suffer when they lack clarity of purpose. Teams also suffer when given unclear assignments. Before creating a team, it is important to define the team's purpose explicitly and also to be clear about what is outside its purpose. If it has already been determined who will be on the team, it can be helpful to have members involved in these conversations.

One of my client congregations set up a team to do a feasibility study for a new elevator. However, in the process of doing their work, the team expanded the scope of its work. They did not seek permission to change their assigned task. The elevator team decided to study a wide variety of building issues facing the congregation. As a result, instead of coming back with a tightly written report on the elevator, they produced a laundry list of expensive projects for the congregation to consider. The congregation's board was so overwhelmed by the larger list that it never got around to focusing on the elevator.

One way to gain clarity about a team's purpose is to imagine what the team will produce in the way of results. In other words, if a team achieves its purpose, what will be the resulting impact? What will be different than if they hadn't done their work? For example, if a team teaching a Sunday school class achieves its purpose, what will be the impact? We can imagine that the children will be filled with enthusiasm for and knowledge about the essentials of our faith; a clear, colorful, engaging classroom; happy parents; happy students; and, yes, happy clergy!

Again, the Sunday school teaching team also needs to know which issues are not its responsibility. If a child is emotionally unhappy, is the team supposed to respond, or is that a larger pastoral care issue for the pastoral staff? If the classroom is not well maintained, should the team clean it, tell the cleaning staff, or let the head of staff know that the cleaners aren't doing their job? If the curriculum is less than engaging, should the team find its own curriculum or turn it over to the Christian education team/committee to resolve it?

When a team is established, those creating it need to sit down with its members and say, "Here is what we want you to do. However, you don't need to get involved in doing this or that. If you are successful, these are the results that we will see." The team members can be asked if they have any questions. Finally, it is wise to ask the team to repeat verbally its assignment to make sure it is understood.

When the team is created and its clarity of purpose established, who will communicate the purpose to the team? Typically, it will be done by the head of staff, a staff member, or a person designated by the governing council. The purpose should be stated in writing so team members can refer to the statement as they engage in their work.

As the story about the "elevator team" reveals, something else should be communicated at the beginning. We want to give teams the autonomy to do their task the way they deem best. However, freedom regarding their method cannot be confused with freedom to change the task. If a team senses that its purpose needs to be expanded or altered, such a possibility is open to discussion. But the decision to change a team's purpose cannot be the result solely of an intra-team talk. If a change is desired, the team must take its opinions to the person or body that created it. If the team's creator agrees to this change the purpose, so be it. If not, it is back to work on the original assignment.

Teams focused on accomplishing their task are a gift to a congregation. Teams focused on figuring out their purpose, not so much! A friend of mine set up a chancel team to manage the setup prior to worship. She thought the purpose was straightforward. Make sure the candles are lit, the sound system is working, the Bible is opened to the right page, worship bulletins are on the chairs of the liturgists, and so on. However, before long, the chancel team came to her wanting to redesign the entire chancel area. After spending months trying to get the team back to its original assignment, my friend now is very, very clear about purpose when she sets up a new team.

TYPES OF TEAMS

Once the purpose and work of a team is established, its creators need to determine what type of team is needed to do the intended work. This is true whether the team is self-creating or started by a staff member or governing body. In their excellent book, *Team Building*, William Dyers and his sons have identified three common types of teams: decision-making, task-accomplishing, or self-directed.[3] Distinguishing between these three different types is an important step in team creation that often goes overlooked. Each of the three types requires distinct competencies from its members.

A strategic planning team is an example of a decision-making team. Members are charged to make decisions about a congregation's vision, establish goals that move the congregation toward the vision, and endorse strategies to realize the goals. Granted, their decisions will need to be ratified by a governing council and perhaps the entire congregation. But they are making decisions that will then be embraced or rejected by others. The large amount of work done by a strategic planning team will certainly make it feel like a task to the members. However, they don't accomplish concrete results such as making sure the chancel is set up correctly for worship every Sunday or teaching a class. A decision-making team may decide to start a new class, but they aren't the task-accomplishing team that will teach it. Decision-making teams are judged by the helpfulness of the choices they make.

A task team, such as a group of ushers, executes well-defined assignments to accomplish a specific purpose. Each member of the team has specific things he or she is supposed to do in order for Sunday morning worship to go smoothly. If any member of the team doesn't perform her or his task, the overall result they seek to accomplish will be compromised. Task-accomplishing team members are judged by how well they carry out their assigned work.

A self-directed team is given a great deal of autonomy by its creator to accomplish its task in ways the team feels best. For example, a congregation's governing council realizes it has been operating without adequate personnel policies. It doesn't know exactly what may be involved in creating new ones. Therefore, it creates a team and tells them to do whatever is necessary to get new, comprehensive policies drafted for the council's review and approval. The council acts with the understanding that the scope of the team's work will unfold and become clear as it gets into its assigned responsibility. The team may choose to be a task team (produce personnel policies) or it may allow individual team members a great deal of freedom to get the job done (e.g., make decisions about whether or not sexual misconduct policies should be included in personnel policies). To a certain degree, the team will decide how it goes about its task and even what its task will be. A self-directed team will be judged by how well it manages the scope of its work as well as the task it accomplishes.

In addition to understanding the type of team needed for a particular assignment, it is also important to be clear as to whether the task is short or long term in nature. A team set up specifically to create personnel policies is a classic short-term assignment. In contrast, a personnel team will handle the long-term responsibility of using the policies as it works with church employees on issues ranging from annual reviews to salary negotiations.

Several of the congregations I have served as a consultant have moved from personnel committees to personnel teams to insure they have the right people to do complicated personnel management work. Healthy teams understand the importance of group dynamics. Given the difficult staffing issues that can arise in a congregation, having a team that attends to its own internal dynamics can be an advantage over a traditional personnel committee.

Long-term teams face the issue of replenishing team members. A committee system usually has terms of service that create an orderly method to replace members who rotate off. In long-term teams, team leaders need to generate periodic discussions about who wants to remain on the team and who wants to leave. As people depart, will the team be given the freedom to seek its own new members, or is there another process the congregation will use to recruit new members? There is no right answer to the question. The important thing is that a clearly defined process is established to allow team members to leave and be replaced by others with similar skill sets and commitments.

AVOIDING THE MICROMANAGEMENT TRAP

J. Richard Hackman writes convincingly about what we covered in chapter 1: "Effective team self-management is impossible unless someone in authority sets the direction for the team's work."[4] However, once direction is set, there is a difficult line leaders must walk. They must ensure that projects are headed in the right direction without micromanaging the team assigned the work.

Making sure a team is doing its job, headed in the right direction, and will complete its task on time are all reasonable expectations. In older models of management, those in authority setting up a team would stay engaged in the team's work. In effect, they became team leaders, making sure that everything was being done properly (as the people in authority understood "properly"). This model works less well in the twenty-first century.

Today, teams expect those in authority to set their direction and perhaps give performance measures with a completion date. They then expect to be left alone to do their work in ways they deem best. If this doesn't happen, the word "micromanage" will quickly come to dominate discussions between teams and a congregation's leadership. Teams charged with carrying out a task will start to wonder, "Well, why don't they just come here and do the work themselves if they want it done their way?"

There are three takeaways regarding management of teams. First, as I cannot say too often, set a clear direction for teams. Without it, they will flounder or create a direction that isn't consistent with what congregational leadership desires. Second, have performance measures for the team. Once a team understands its task and decides on a method of accomplishing the assignment, I suggest allowing it to set its own performance measures and timelines. Teams can share their performance measures with the congregation's leadership to make sure they are acceptable. Following this path for performance measurements removes an argument some-where down the line that goes like this:

> *Congregational Leader*: We gave you some performance meas-ures, and you haven't achieved them.

> *Team Members*: Frankly, you never asked us if we thought the performance measures were reasonable or wise. If you had asked us, we would have told you that they are not reasonable. We could have given you some doable metrics.

Allowing teams to set their own performance measures is empower-ing. It says to a team, "We trust you to do the job."

Third, once direction is set, leave the team alone. It is a good idea to establish a timetable for check-ins with the team to see how they are doing. But the meetings, at least initially, aren't about per-formance as such. In early meetings, the questions from congrega-tional leadership to team members will be along the lines of, "Is the direction we set clear? Does it need to be modified? Do you have the resources, especially the people and financial, you need to ac-complish your work? Is there anything we can do to help you? Would you like to share with us where you are on the project?" These types of questions exhibit a management style intent on want-ing a team to succeed rather than messages loaded with tacit impli-cations that management is worried the group may not be doing its job. Again, the questions asked will be an indication of trust or lack of such in the team's ability to handle its work.

Hackman summarizes the different responsibilities of those creating the team from those who are members of the team when he writes, "To foster self-managing, goal-directed work, those who create work teams should be insistent and unapologetic about exer-cising their authority to specify end states, but equally insistent about not specifying the details of the means by which the team is to pursue those ends."[5] When leaders set direction for a team, then demonstrate trust in team members to take appropriate actions, there is an energizing ripple effect. The team will feel empowered as it realizes that it is truly free to do the work as it deems best. Equally important, team members will feel as though their work matters, since it is being entrusted to them. In contrast, when there is unclear direction or micromanagement, a team feels disempowered, and the members usually disengage from their task.

Hackman frames the relationship of the team to its creator (governing board or staff person) in terms of ends and means.[6] Creators of teams make clear the end they want accomplished. They leave the means to a particular end to the teams. I think it is a brilliantly simple paradigm to remember as we work in congregations. Leaders need to remind themselves that they are all about defining the ends. Teams need to remind themselves that they are all about the means to the desired outcome.

In a team-driven congregation, the governing board and staff assume the leadership function, while teams are given the management function. What do effective managers do? There are thousands of books on this subject. From the literature and my own personal experience, the key functions of managers include focusing on short-term results by engaging in detailed planning and disciplined execution, problem solving as surprises appear that were not anticipated, and creating orderly processes. When the direction is set, a team should immediately move into a managerial mode. They will create a plan to handle their task and execute it. My contention is that teams are able to handle the management function in most congregations far better than any clergy or governing board. The latter two should be engaged in the leadership function, not management.

Hackman has a keen insight for those creating teams. When leaders set clear purpose, he writes, "good direction for a task-performing team is clear—but also incomplete."[7] Indeed, to the extent that the task is overly defined, leaders have micromanaged before the team even goes to work.

Remember Pink's motivators? One of them was mastery. Why did he recommend a focus on helping people achieve mastery of a particular skill? Because it is an open-ended goal. We can never fully master our craft. A team can totally master its assignment. To the extent that there is an open-ended, incomplete aspect to the direction-setting by congregational leadership, the team will have the freedom to think of and to do things leadership never considered. When a team's assignment is too tightly defined by those creating the team, the team members will feel like robots—simply doing that which they were preprogrammed to accomplish. The use of robots in manufacturing works wonderfully in the car industry. Trying to make church members into robots doesn't work so well!

Early in my ministry at Western Presbyterian Church, I was not satisfied with the manner in which the congregation's building was being cleaned. As I was young and inexperienced at managing people, I used a totally inappropriate strategy in my attempt to improve the situation. I opted for micromanagement. I spoke several times with the janitor and explained to him areas where I would like to see improvement in the cleaning. When I didn't see better results, I decided to create a highly detailed list of things for the janitor to do and the exact time frames during the day when I wanted them done. As I now know, my strategy was a model of what not to do.

A wise, gentle man, the janitor followed my instructions to the "t," and the church soon looked less clean than it had previously. He, of course, knew that it would be less clean but let me discover it for myself. Clearly, my micromanaging of his schedule was not having the desired impact. So the janitor and I had another discussion. First, I profusely apologized to him for intruding in his work area. Second, I reminded him that the church needed to be cleaner than it had been in the past. Finally, I said, "It is your job to make sure this building is clean, not mine. So again, I apologize for micromanaging your work. I will let you do your job, and I will return to my job. My job does not include micromanaging *how* the building gets cleaned, but my job does include ensuring that this place *is* clean. I leave the means to that end up to you. If that end isn't met, we'll have other discussions until it is accomplished."

Gaston and I had a wonderful working relationship for the next thirty years. By the way, the ultimate solution to our cleaning problems came a number of years later when we were able to free up enough money to hire a part-time cleaning person. At that point, Gaston was able to focus on working with our contractors to maintain the building's HVAC, plumbing, and other large systems. It was work for which he had passion and better skills.

Micromanaging an employee and micromanaging a team are fruits of the same tree. Each displays a lack of trust in the ability of the employee/team to get work done. If we want teams to succeed in our congregations, we have to trust them to do their work. When describing her success as a business leader at Yahoo, Google, and Change.org, Jennifer Dulski said, "I became good at setting clear direction for the team. Even when we were working with a larger company, we still did things like agree on our values as a team, the mission, vision and clear priorities."[8] She said she learned the importance and power of teamwork as a coxswain for her high school's rowing team. If congregational leaders set a clear direction for teams *and* leave it up to the team to accomplish its mission as they deem best, teams will thrive in our congregations. If we are either too precise or too imprecise in our direction-setting, our teams will struggle.

PULLING THE TEAM TOGETHER

Congregations, like many other organizations, tend to think that if they determine clarity of purpose, build a solid strategic plan, and have their plan reasonably financed that they are good to go. However, if the congregation doesn't have the right people in place, staff and volunteers, to implement the plan, the expected results will not be forthcoming. Having the right people on the team, whether it be a staff team, lay leadership team, or work teams, is the single most important ingredient to success. A team can be given clear direction and the resources it needs to do the job. However, if the right people aren't on the team, it will not succeed.

As mentioned earlier, too often, congregations put together teams using criteria unrelated to the assigned task. For example, unless the team's work requires a representation of all the congregation's interest groups to succeed, creating a representative team is irrelevant. What matters is having the correct skill sets and personality types on the team to get the very specific task done.

The most challenging of the various criteria sometimes used to staff teams has to do with pastoral care. We often put a person on a team not because they have the appropriate skill set but because we think they need to be on a team to improve their spiritual, emotional, or mental health. They are recruited not because it will be good for the team but because it will be good for them personally. For the team to succeed and the person to enjoy the team experience, it has to be good for both the team and the individual.

As a pastor for forty years, I totally understand the desire to think about pastoral care concerns when selecting team members. I would see a person who was grieving the death of her husband and think, "I wonder if putting her to work on a team would help her develop a new source of energy for her life?" Or I would see a person who was angry at the church and contemplate, "What if I brought him 'inside the tent' by giving him some responsibility of a team?" Putting such people on a team sometimes helped them overcome their particular challenge. More often, it did not.

As for the team itself, placing a person on a team because of pastoral care concerns does not necessarily help it perform to its highest potential. The grieving person may be so deep in grief that she can't contribute to the team. The angry congregational member may just become an angry team member.

Pastoral concerns plus team needs can come together in a win-win. If a team needs an excellent analyst of data while a grieving husband or angry member happens to be good at this work, the team can be made stronger. When this happens, the team experience enables the grieving or angry person to move to a different place emotionally. Nonetheless, such convergences, while wonderful, should not be expected to happen automatically. When creating a team, the primary consideration is not a congregational member's emotional health. The focus has to stay on what the team needs to be successful.

The individuals who recruit team members are also key to finding the right people to make an effective group. Their understanding of what a team needs is so important. Typically a church governing body of some type or staff member will pick team members, unless the entity is self-forming. I am inclined to think that the smaller the group choosing team members, the more likely the task will stay focused on the team's needs rather than devolving into considerations such as "Who isn't doing anything right now who we can ask to serve on this team?"

As a pastor, how many times did I make the mistake of asking the following question of my congregation's governing board? "Ok, so we have decided to create a (you name it) team. Who do you think we can get to serve on it?" Too many times I got the following inappropriate responses: "Well, Jane and Larry's kids just went off to college. They are empty nesters. It would be good for them to get involved in something," or "Jerry is totally out of place on the worship committee. Maybe he would do better on this team," or "We have to find a place for Sara. She is always complaining. Let's bring her 'inside the tent' by putting her on this new team." When we followed that approach, we chose team members for all the wrong reasons. Using the same type of criteria while continuing a faulty line of reasoning, we then tried to figure out who would be the chair. "Well, Jane has lots of time on her hands. Let's make her chair."

Rather than going through this all-too-familiar process, I suggest that one or two people be charged with pulling together a team. They should be people who understand the issues outlined in this book regarding how one creates a team. These team recruiters can focus on finding people with the particular skills and personality traits needed for each team. Creating such a group without the requisite skill sets and team-player personalities is a certain recipe for an ineffective outcome.

The literature on teams produces lots of different characteristics we should look for when putting one together. I particularly like the Dyers' list, which recommends finding team members with:

- The skills or knowledge needed to do the assigned task
- Good interpersonal and communication skills
- A commitment to working in/as a team
- A demonstrated ability to adapt to things as the team faces unexpected challenges and opportunities
- The gift of dependability
- An ability to take initiative within the team [9]

While possessing the required skill set is crucial, the second and third characteristics on the list are routinely undervalued in the recruitment of team members. Skills can overcome a lack of interpersonal skills in certain instances. For example, a congregation creates a team to revamp its computer network. A prickly personality who has incredible computer networking skills may be worth the difficulties he creates on the team if no one else with similar skills is available. Without the person, the team will probably fail.

However, there are some people who are team players and some who are not. Putting a "lone ranger" on a team is an invitation for team dysfunction. In like manner, there are some people who have the personality and communication skills to work through conflict and some who don't. If a team doesn't have a few people who know how to manage conflict, the team will suffer when conflict inevitably occurs. We will talk more about this in chapter 3.

Many congregations in the United States have a relatively homogeneous makeup. People seem inclined to join faith communities that have approaches to life similar to their own. As a result, historically, congregations have tended to have similar demographics when it comes to race and economic class.

Hackman has an important insight on how the issue of homogeneity can impact the creation of a team. He writes, "Members of excessively homogeneous groups may get along well together but lack the full complement of resources needed to perform well. An excessively heterogeneous group may have a rich diversity of talent and perspective but be unable to use it well because members are too different in how they think and behave."[10] The smaller the congregation, the more difficult it may be to address the homogeneity factor in assembling a team. However, in larger congregations, attention should be paid to it.

A lack of intergenerational diversity within a congregation can be particularly problematic for creating effective, vital teams. The millennial generation is the largest in our nation. Polling data shows that they have significant preferences that differ from the gen Xers and baby boomers. For example, they are more inclined to be optimistic about the future than other generations. Failing to bring the millennial perspective into a team's membership robs the team of key insights that will make the team more effective.

I was on a team where the millennial team members kept reminding the baby boomers that our style of communicating would fail if directed at their generation. For example, baby boomers, who expect questions to be answered thoroughly, will push until they are satisfied with the responses. Given their positive orientation toward life, millennials can find the boomer approach as overly critical and contentious.[11] Being sensitive to the millennial generation's values, we ended up communicating decisions or actions to the larger congregation in ways that included the communication preferences of younger generations. We used email, asked for feedback from those receiving the emails, and used a respectful tone. Since the larger organization's membership was over one-third millennials, we would have had major communication issues without millennials on the team. In addition to creating demographic diversity, their knowledge of millennial communication patterns was an extremely valuable skill set.

It is crucial to remember that not every church member is a potentially good team player. Some of us are better off working by ourselves. Putting nonteam types on a team will frustrate everyone involved and sabotage the team. I once heard an executive say that he knows a team is dysfunctional when he observes five team members focusing their energy on getting one member to be a good team player.

After finding individuals with the right qualities for a particular team and before finalizing their selection, it is important for a person skilled in team dynamics to step back and look at the team as a whole. Imagine them working together. Will they work together? If the answer is yes, the team can be formed.

I don't like to use sports metaphors. But team sports do provide some valuable insights into team behavior and dysfunction. In football, occasionally a team will release an extremely skilled player because he isn't a team player. There are many instances of all-pro players being cut or traded because their inability to be good teammates outweighs their high productivity at their particular position.

Think about that. It is more important to many professional sports teams that members be good team players than highly skilled ones. As we put together teams in our congregations, we need to keep this example in mind. We want team members with excellent skills. However, we also want those who are either instinctively good team players or are willing to learn how to become good at this.

TEAM SIZE

How many people make for an effective team? There is an enormous amount of literature about the right size of a team. Most experts say the tendency is to create a team that is too large, not too small. We think more is better. However, research reveals that the optimum team size is five to seven individuals. Amazon favors what it calls "two pizza" teams—small enough that two pizzas can feed the team. The larger the team, the more difficult it is to realize a common agreement on how and what work should be done. There is some flexibility with that number.

Considerable research reveals the counterintuitive fact that teams with more than twelve members experience a serious decline in effectiveness.[12] Using the "more hands on deck" approach, we are inclined to think that adding more people to a team will speed up the pace of the work. Frederick Brooks, a systems manager at IBM, developed what has become known as Brooks's Law. The law states that adding manpower to a project already underway tends to make the project come in later rather than on time. Psychologist Ivan Steiner's research confirmed Brooks's Law. He shows that as we add people to a team, each person adds less productivity than the previous person. So, for example, when we increase a team from three to four, the fourth person adds much more to the effectiveness and efficiency of the team than does the thirteenth person added to a twelve-member team. As important, Steiner shows that productivity actually begins to decrease when the team grows to more than five members. The sixth person decreases productivity. The seventh person decreases it even more! Drop-offs in productivity become more significant after the seventh person is added, which is why the experts prefer teams of five to seven members. [13]

Does this research challenge conventional wisdom in a congregation or what? Many people think that the more people we have doing something, the better. In fact, such an assumption seems to be totally wrong. The issue involves recruiting five to seven people who have the skills and team-savvy personalities needed for the team to work well. In some instances, a particular task may require the team size to increase to twelve. For example, at a feeding program for the homeless, the daily team required to feed 250 individuals may be larger than seven. But too often I see the larger size exception becoming the rule. The business community, US military forces, and others have researched the size issue thoroughly. When creating teams, congregations need to respect the findings of the research.

Small teams can also make a large or even midsize congregation seem more intimate. Many people I know who attend megachurches talk about the teams and small groups where they spend most of their time. They say that their teams and small groups personalize what can be a less-than-personal worship experience.

Early on, the technology industry learned the value of using teams. As companies such as Microsoft and Google grew bigger, they turned to small teams to keep productivity high while giving employees a relatively intimate work environment. In like manner, a large congregation can maintain high productivity in its ministry with the use of teams.

Keeping team sizes in the range of five to seven members demands discipline. A congregation mobilizing its membership through teams needs an ongoing educational effort to inform members about how and why teams work. When reasonable people understand that team size matters, they are likely to accept the need for teams with small memberships.

I worked recently with a large urban congregation that has followed Alban Senior Consultant Dan Hotchkiss's advice on the size of its governing board.[14] A several-thousand-member congregation has created a governing council of nine individuals. The idea is that this small church council will be more productive and effective than its very large predecessor. In effect, the congregation has chosen to be led by a team rather than a larger governing body. The size is slightly over the optimum team size, but close enough to the norm. Members are chosen for specific governance skill sets they bring to the board. They work to nurture a positive team dynamic. I know of several other congregations that have made a similar transition to a team-size governing board.

The transition to the smaller governing team has not been seamless. Transitions never are. In this case, some members are resisting, believing that a larger governing board is more representative of the congregation as a whole. "Can a team of nine represent a congregation?" the critics ask. However, in my opinion, a more appropriate question is, "Can a team of nine built on the leadership qualities of its members or a large body built on representational principles best lead a congregation?"

The strength of the US House of Representatives is its ability to reflect a membership that mirrors the various factions in our society. However, its representative nature has increasingly crippled its ability to make decisions. Not wanting to betray their constituents, each representative votes for the small rather than big picture. The advantage of a nonrepresentative leadership team in a congregation is that it can lead from the perspective of a big picture, not from that of a bunch of smaller pictures.

There are strengths and weaknesses in both a representative model and a team model. For our time and place, the team model seems to have become more popular in corporations, nonprofits, and some congregations. Would it work in your congregation?

TIME FRAME

When establishing a team with a task that needs to be done by a certain date, it is wise to create a timeline. When does the team need to be finished? When should the team report to its creators about progress being or not being made? What results will be produced if the team has successfully finished its task? I recommend allowing the team to define its own timeline. If they create one that is unacceptable, a dialogue can then take place between the team and its managers/creators until a mutually agreeable timeline is in place. The creation of the timeline is also a good opportunity to have a team create performance measures for itself. Again, if the measures are unacceptable to those who create the team, a dialogue can find common ground.

TEAM LEADERS

Hopefully we are realizing that moving to teams is a process that requires much thought. There needs to be a clear sense of purpose, the leaders of a congregation need to avoid micromanaging teams, and considerable attention needs to be paid to picking the right team members, ensuring the team is the right size and making sure team members have the resources required to do their work. With all of that in place, we have more work to do if teams are to be successful. Namely, we need to support team leaders.

How does team leadership emerge? In some instances, a team leader is designated by the person/group responsible for establishing the team. In other instances, the team shares the leadership function among all members or picks one of its members to be the leader. Both models have their own strengths. The key is not so much which model is used but for a team to know who its leader is.

In the appointed leader model, it is clear who the leader is. When teams adopt a shared leadership model, leadership usually rotates as the task demands. For example, in a teaching team in a Sunday school, one person may have excellent knowledge of the material being taught. She becomes the leader when the discussion is on understanding the material. Another member may have excellent teaching skills. He becomes the leader in discussions about teaching style. A third member may have good negotiating skills. She becomes the leader when the team asks the congregation's governing board for more money to buy books, furniture, or other supplies. When rotating leadership, one person is designated leader for a specific time or until a specific aspect of work is completed. In other words, team members will always be able to say, "Person X is our team leader at the present time."

In a *Harvard Business Review* book, Linda Gratton and Tamara J. Erickson describe the results of their research in "Eight Ways to

Build Collaborative Teams."[15] They note that there is much debate in the business and research communities about the most appropriate style for leading a team as the designated team leader. Some argue that individuals with great people skills are the best team leaders. Others suggest that individuals with a strong task orientation are best.

Studying fifty-five teams, Gratton and Erickson found that there is truth in both positions.[16] In fact, they discovered that the most effective team leaders tend to shift gears as tasks change or new tasks emerge. Gregory Huszczo agrees with this conclusion in his book on team leadership.[17] Gifted team leaders start with a strong task orientation to make sure that team members are focused on their assigned responsibilities. Once direction is established, they switch to a relationship orientation, helping to maintain a healthy sense of team as the work begins to wear on team members, individually and collectively. As the project reaches its conclusion, we can imagine the leader reverting back to a primarily task orientation to make sure issues get wrapped up properly. One participant in their study, Marriott Corporation, offers in-house training for team leaders to create these "ambidextrous" skills of task orientation and relationship building.

Huszczo makes the point that "the essence in a team environment is influence, not control."[18] Following Gratton's and Erickson's insights, this means a team leader will find ways to motivate team members to stay focused on their responsibilities. Midcourse, the team leader will find ways build a sense of team by inspiring members to work together and encouraging them to overcome difficulties as a group rather than facing them individually. One can argue for an emphasis on team building from the beginning. However, in my experience, we learn how to be a team while we are a team.

J. Richard Hackman provides a helpful list of the various skills a team leader needs to develop.[19] *Envisioning skill* relates to a leader's ability to articulate the team's purpose so it remains at the core of their work. *Inventive skill* involves appreciating that there are many ways to get a job done. The team leader can nurture creative approaches to the team's work. *Negotiating skill* is required both within the team as it works through conflict and with the organization that created the team to get the resources needed to complete the job. *Decision-making skill* is necessary to make sure that the team makes timely choices rather than endlessly debating options. *Teaching skill* is an asset as the leader shows teammates how to accomplish what they don't know about while being a team. *Interpersonal skill* is necessary to create a cohesive team culture. *Implementation skill* helps the leader follow through on all the details needed for any project to be successful.

Very few individuals possess all of these skills. As one establishes a team, it is important to understand which of the skills will be most important to accomplish the assigned task. The person/group setting up the team can then find someone in the congregation with the right skill set to be leader.

COACHING

Pastor Jones set up a team to plan a capital campaign to build a new educational wing for the congregation's growing religious education program. Working with her governing board, she established a clear purpose (crucially distinguishing the capital campaign's work from that of the ongoing stewardship committee) and recruited a group of six people with the right skill set. She named a member with both good fundraising and people skills to be the team leader. Finally, she said, "Go to it." In about three months, Pastor Jones began hearing stories about the team being dysfunctional—conflict among members, confusion about who was doing what, and complaints from team members that they didn't have the resources needed to do their work.

Pastor Jones's mistake was classic. She rightly didn't want to micromanage, so she told the group to go ahead with their work. However, coaching a team and its leader isn't micromanaging. In my consulting work, I have begun to do a good bit of coaching of clergy who need various kinds of help and support as they do their ministry. As a consultant, I often serve as a coach to governing boards and planning teams. As a coach, my job is not to get knee-deep into their work. My function is to support them by telling them about best practices that are effective elsewhere, pointing them to resources that broaden their perspective on a particular issue, helping them to see problems they may not see, and encouraging them when the going gets tough. When I am coaching, I don't even come close to telling my clients what to do. They make the decisions to do the ministry. I support them as best I can.

In like manner, team leaders and teams generally need some coaching (being a sympathetic listener as the leader deals with problems, suggesting alternate ways to get something done, and so on) as they go about their work, especially in the early phase of their work together. A failure to provide quality coaching increases the chance that a team will fail in its task. After creating the building campaign team, Pastor Jones needed to move into a coaching role with the team. Huszczo says the goal is to develop a "coaching style that enlightens, educates and expands a team's thinking, not one that dictates and controls."[20] Fearing being labeled a micromanager, too many managers avoid engagement with their teams altogether. Again, coaching is not micromanaging. If it becomes micromanaging, it is no longer coaching.

Skilled coaches give people the help they need when they ask for it. Sometimes we need to ask teams if they need help, because they won't ask for help. Growing up in Wisconsin in the middle of the twentieth century, I was in a culture where asking for help was widely viewed as a sign of weakness. As a result, we didn't ask for coaching.

As a novice assistant pastor in Houston, I came under criticism because I didn't respond appropriately to a couple whose house had flooded. In fact, I had called them. But the couple never said a word about the flood. I, stupidly, didn't ask! When I got criticized, I called them and said, "I called you right after the flood, and you didn't say a word about it." They responded, "You didn't ask." Point. Counterpoint. In this book, the point is that sometimes we need to ask teams if they need any assistance. If we don't, they may never tell us.

What might Pastor Jones have done to coach the capital campaign team? First things first, the pastor could have asked the team if they had everything they needed to do their work. Perhaps they lacked some specific skills needed to do their job. Jones might have suggested that outside fundraising specialists could be hired to help the team if they desired or maybe added another team member who possessed the missing skill or knowledge. If the team lacked motivation, Jones could have sat down with the team to explain how crucial their success would be for the future of the congregation. Linking people to a higher purpose is a terrific way to motivate people. Or as the team struggled to hit their fundraising goals, Pastor Jones might have made some suggestions: "By the way, have you paid a visit on Bill and Marcia Smith? They are big contributors to the general budget and have expressed enthusiasm for the new education wing being built."

No team member could interpret any of this type of coaching as intrusive or distrustful. It is a clear attempt to support the team as it goes about its work. Healthy teams like coaching as they go about their work. If a team doesn't welcome coaching, they have adopted the highly individualistic approach to work that has dominated US society historically. They are similar to an individual who thinks he needs no help.

Rose's Luxury restaurant has become the hot spot to eat in Washington, DC. An article in the *Washington Post* describes the teamwork that fuels Rose's success:

> [Aaron] Silverman, 32, has quietly undermined the traditional role of head chef at his laid-back restaurant on Barracks Row, where he has racked up praise and honors with the apparent ease of getting wet in the rain. In a town where collaboration is considered a weakness, and in a hospitality industry where kitchen hierarchy remains as fixed as true north, Silverman believes in the collective creative power of his cooks, not to mention his managers, servers, bartenders and everyone else. They all have a voice, and they all are free to express it. [21]

First, note the age of the owner. Silverman, at age thirty-two, is in the demographic that finds teamwork to be the most effective and satisfying way to realize its goals. Second, Silverman has, in effect, become a coach to his staff. He encourages the creativity within the team, helps them get the resources they need as he fosters a collective, collegial decision-making process. This is how Apple, Google, and so many other cutting-edge companies are making millions of dollars. Can congregations employ a similar approach to serving God, as well as their members and communities? Yes.

CONCLUSION

In this chapter, I have attempted to show the importance of setting up a team to succeed. If we simply pull together a group of people or allow them to pull themselves together, research from the business community shows that the possibility of team failure increases exponentially, in contrast to those that are established with a sense of intentionality and accountability. In a congregation, whoever is responsible for creating a team—whether it is a staff person, governing board, or committee—needs to go through the steps we have described for creating a successful team.

First, there needs to be a clear understanding of the team's purpose. What is the team supposed to do? What will the results look like if the team is successful? This needs to be communicated to the team at the beginning of its life and then reiterated as the team does its work.

Second, those establishing the team need to be clear about what type of team is needed. Will the team be asked primarily to make decisions about something? Will it be a very task-oriented charge? Or will the team be self-directed, allowed to find its way as it works? From the beginning, each team needs to know the nature and ramifications of that decision. Task-oriented teams, for example, are not supposed to be making many decisions about the nature of their task. They are intended to perform the task.

Third, keeping the team size small is crucial. Big teams tend to bog down productivity because they aren't agile enough to make decisions quickly. This size goes back to the adage of "too many cooks in the kitchen." In a major, counterintuitive finding, research shows the more members we add to a team, the lower its productivity becomes.

Fourth, the group or individual setting up the team needs to avoid micromanaging. At the same time, the team's creators need to be clear that they are available to coach and will check in regularly to see if help is needed. The team and its creator need to agree not just on the purpose of the team but also on performance measures by which they can determine if the purpose was realized.

Fifth, team leadership and the type of leadership need to be identified. Is it one person selected by the creator of the team? Does leadership rotate based on the task being done at the time? Or does the team select its own leader(s)? All options can work, but it needs to be clear which option is being employed.

Sixth, most coaches need teams. Great coaches know when to intervene, when to stay out of the way. They know how to nurture and, at times, push for improvement. Congregational teams need coaches. The coach will usually be a staff person.

When all of these factors are taken into account in the creation of a team, we have a group of people whose chance of having an optimum team experience has been significantly enhanced. To the people who say "yes" to an invitation to serve on a team, we owe the best chance at succeeding. Following the steps in this chapter creates that best chance.

3

CREATING A HEALTHY TEAM

As an adult, my first intense team experience came in my executive MBA program at George Washington University in Washington, DC. We were put together in a team by the dean, who made team assignments based on geographic location, thinking that if we lived near each other, it would be easier for us to meet. Our team ended up being male and female, gay and straight, liberal and conservative politically. We worked in the church, government, private sector, and hospitals. Since my teammates were all in their thirties and I was in my early fifties, generational differences were also a factor in our team dynamics.

Some people have affairs when they have a midlife crisis. I have found pursuing educational degrees to being a healthier response to midlife self-questioning! Feeling stale and looking forward to the twenty-first century, in 2000, I went looking for a challenge. Since I was never good at math, I thought the finance, accounting, and other math components of the executive MBA program would be a good way to get my creative juices flowing.

After enrolling, I discovered that one-half of my final grades in each class would be based on grades I received while doing team assignments. Since I am very grade conscious and competitive, I am not sure I would have enrolled had I known about the team grade being so important. But it was too late to turn back. So there I was with four strangers in a challenging program trying to figure out how to work with teammates much younger than me.

It didn't take long for me to notice that each of us was doing A-quality work on our individual assignments and tests, while our group work tended to be on the B to B+ level. In these MBA programs, one quickly discovers that a B is basically a C. We were doing average work as a team. I don't suffer silently, so I let my teammates know that I was dissatisfied with our low team grades. They acknowledged the problem, but we never made understanding and solving the issue a priority. We were too busy trying to get our assignments done while working full-time, demanding jobs.

In our team meetings, I kept mentioning our lower grade performance, and we started to argue about it. When the dean heard about some contentiousness in our team, he asked us to meet with him. At the meeting, the dean said, "So why are you arguing with each other? What is the problem?" My teammates all looked at me and said, "John is the problem. He keeps harping on the fact that our team grades are lower than our individual grades." The dean responded, "John, is that true?" I said, "Absolutely. I find it unacceptable." At that point, the argument broke out in front of the dean.

In less than a half hour, the dean was able to help us understand some of the problems that were causing us to underperform as a team. Since we had only known each other for a few months, we were reluctant to criticize each other's work. Rather than critically editing each other's work to create a quality, seamless paper, we simply took each person's work, pasted it into a single document, and handed it in. No one said, "John, I don't think your segment is thorough," or "Jane, I don't agree with your conclusions about the data we gathered." We didn't want to offend each other by asking tough questions about our work.

In addition, we had one teammate who chronically handed in work at the last minute. We had to nag him to get papers in to us, but we never challenged him on his tardiness. Again, we didn't want to offend a teammate.

Finally, as a team, we didn't seem to care about the quality of our work. We were satisfied getting it done, not getting it done well. As a result, our team papers and projects lacked the quality that was present in our individual work, which had our name attached to it.

Following our cathartic meeting with the dean, our team behavior changed dramatically. We started a very rigorous editing process prior to handing in the final product. We gave each other permission to criticize anything and everything. The point was no longer whether one of us got criticized. The goal was to produce a high-quality piece of work. Our grades moved up to the A level. We were happier with one another. Other teams began to ask us what we were doing to get such high grades.

As I have studied teams, I now understand that the MBA program did a lot of things wrong when it came to setting up our teams. As we discussed in the last chapter, it is a recipe for dysfunctional teams to set them up randomly (in this case, by geography), not give teams clear instructions about how to function as a team, and not provide ongoing coaching to a team. The fact that some of the other teams were high functioning was a reflection of the fact that many of the younger students were used to working in teams in their workplaces. As a result, they knew what to do to make their team function well.

There are many ways to analyze the processes that teams go through as they do their work. As a way of illustrating what a congregation can expect in the way of team management, I am going to apply several analytical tools for team dynamics to my MBA experience. Hopefully, it will help readers understand both the phases teams go through as well as the unique management and coaching tasks each phase requires. Having a healthy team is not an accident. It is the result of congregational leadership and team members paying attention to the quality of team life.

THE TURKMAN PARADIGM

The paradigm that applies best to our MBA team is very old, having been created by psychologist Bruce Turkman back in 1965.[1] He describes the exact stages our MBA team went through during the program. Turkman lays out a process in which teams *form, storm, norm, perform*, and *adjourn*. Much of the last chapter discussed the formation period in which teams are selected, the work assignment is explained, and performance measures may be detailed.

In the formation period, team members are overly polite to one another, not wanting to rock the new boat. This is exactly what happened with my MBA team. We differed with one another on many of the complex academic issues before us as a team. However, afraid of creating conflict, we never discussed our differences. We simply accepted whatever a teammate contributed to a group paper or project.

The storming period started before we met in the dean's office. While I was the identified initiator of the conflict, in fact, it had been simmering for weeks in offline conversations between individual team members. The storming continued for a number of weeks after our meeting with the dean, who, in effect, gave us permission to have some healthy arguments in the group as a whole. In that storming period, we learned how to disagree with one another. Fortunately, we also discovered that we liked each other even as we disagreed.

Our arguments led to the creation of group norms. We made commitments to do our assigned work in a timely manner; a few of

ate the norms needed to be effective. As a result, too many teams
to move into the phase of effective performance.

In congregational teams, the fear of conflict is an omnipresent
tor. However, conflict seems to be an unavoidable part of a faith
rney. We see a lot of interpersonal conflict among the Hebrew
ple in their sojourn from slavery to freedom; read in the Gospels
ut conflict between Jesus and his disciples as well as between
disciples themselves; and study major conflicts in the church
h as the establishment of the Nicene Creed or the Protestant
formation. And yet, despite seeing the redemptive role such con-
t has played in our faith traditions, we usually run from it in our
gregations.

HE EXPECTATION MODEL

st people do not come to church hoping or even expecting to
gage in conflict. They want their family of faith to be a safe place
ere they don't have the hassles and criticism they face in the
rkplace and even in their families. However, many of us do not
derstand or believe that safe places are not necessarily conflict-
e places.

A potential spin-off benefit of the use of teams is that congrega-
nal members can learn to disagree with members of their team.
members learn to process conflict in teams, is it reasonable to
ect that they will do better at processing conflict in larger con-
gational settings? I think so. Healthy team behavior can be an
ubator for healthy congregational behavior.

The Dyers maintain that the least helpful way of looking at intra-
m conflict is to view it as the result of personality clashes.[4]
rsonalizing debates over issues leads to the conclusion that some-
e on the team has to either change their personality or leave the

us became editors and were given the authority to make final decisions on what was submitted; and several team members were designated to use their skills with software such as Excel and Power-
Point. When norms were violated, we created a policy that anyone
could name the violation, and we would have a team meeting to
resolve the issue. Finally, we agreed that disagreements were not to
be avoided; they were to be worked through. Because of our newly
created norms, we never reached a meltdown crisis again.

As the norms were created, our performance improved dramatically. Professors and fellow students commented on it. We became
very task oriented. When our work was done after eighteen intense
months, our team adjourned. We remain in touch with each other to
this day.

Tuckman's paradigm is very easy to remember. It is a great
teaching device as teams are set up in congregations. I find it extremely useful as a coach or team leader to say, "We are now engaged in classic storming behavior," or whichever other phase the
team is in. There is something about knowing that all healthy, creative teams go through these five phases that makes them more acceptable and tolerable. The fact that our team argued didn't mean
we were out of control. It meant we were in the storming phase.

In many ways, Tuckman's phases remind me of the grieving
phases developed by Elizabeth Kubler-Ross: denial, anger, bargain-
ing, depression, and acceptance.[2] A person who has experienced a
death can get stuck in the denial phase. It is healthy to experience
denial, unhealthy to get stuck in the denial phase of grieving. As a
congregational leader and manager of teams, what I need to be
concerned about is not a team that is storming. Storming is normal
team behavior. What I need to watch for is a team that gets stuck in
a phase such as storming. When stuck, I need to help teams understand the need to move beyond storming to norming.

How do we move from the storm to the norm? A coach, like our dean, helps us name the problems generating the storm. We then talk through possible solutions to the problems. Finally, we embrace one of the solutions. If it is something we will encounter again, the solution can be named a norm.

THE LENCIONI PARADIGM

Another way to analyze a team's behavior is to use Patrick Lencioni's now famous five dysfunctions of a team.[3] In his fabulous book, Lencioni tells a story in which a corporate management team is dysfunctional because of an absence of trust, fear of conflict, lack of commitment, avoidance of accountability, and inattention to results. As I will explain in the next chapter, I think these also happen to be the five dysfunctions of a congregation.

When our MBA team came together, we didn't know each other. As important, for better or worse, we knew that we had to work together for the next eighteen months. Therefore, in retrospect, it isn't surprising that we didn't trust each other enough to engage in healthy conflict over our team projects. Trust is earned. Only as our team worked, argued, and accomplished tasks together would we learn to trust each other.

It is easy to see how Lencioni's various dysfunctions flow in and out of each other, how interwoven with one another they are. Using my MBA team as an example, we feared conflict, which caused us to avoid holding one another accountable, which meant, ultimately, we didn't pay enough attention to the results (our lower grades). If teammates effectively hold each other accountable, they will inevitably come into conflict. If a team member isn't doing what needs to be done to get the desired results, someone has to hold the teammate

accountable for poor work. Naming the obvious will pr[...] angry sparks.

Lack of commitment manifested itself in a couple [...] our team, one person clearly did not feel a need to produ[...] a timely manner. But none of us were committed en[...] team's success to push performance issues that neede[...] dressed. Yes, I complained about our lower grades but [...] what the dean did and ask, "What is the problem, and [...] solve it?"

In our team, the primary issue was fear of conflict. W[...] ly liked each other and didn't want to rock our fragile [...] as a team. Unwittingly, by avoiding appropriate confli[...] mal differences of opinion, we ensured that conflict [...] place.

So each of Lencioni's five dysfunctions were pr[...] team. However, they were so interwoven with each oth[...] hard to tell which of them was the presenting issue at a[...] in time. As I have worked more with teams, I find th[...] norm. A team doesn't work through Lencioni's five [...] the way a team moves through Tuckman's phases [...] Lencioni's dysfunctions are swirling about within ea[...] man's stages.

Putting Tuckman's and Lencioni's paradigms toget[...] powerful insights into team behavior and what is requir[...] healthy team. Tuckman rightly sees the storming phase[...] the development of a team. Through a series of tou[...] inducing conversations, a team is able to create its [...] Lencioni does a commendable job of describing the fea[...] that, in effect, keeps many teams from ever explicitly [...] storming phase. Afraid of conflict, we avoid it. Attemp[...] conflict, we create subliminal conflict that usually su[...] helpful ways. Not getting through the storming phas[...]

team. The person identified with the personality problem immediately and understandably will become defensive. So the scenario quickly becomes a lose-lose for the team.

Jane called her pastor at St. Michael's Church saying that she urgently needed to talk with her. When she sat down with Pastor Carol, Jane explained that her Sunday school teaching team had become unbearable. "I simply can't work with James anymore. He doesn't prepare his teaching assignments, choosing to wing it in the classroom. He bristles whenever I or anyone else makes suggestions about how the class should run. In my opinion, he has an anger management problem. He is unbearable. You are going to have to replace me or James on the sixth grade teaching team. I won't continue to work with him."

Instead of viewing the sixth grade teaching team through the lens of personality clashes, a better approach, say the Dyers, is to see conflict as the result of a violation of expectations. Jane expected certain things to happen, and they didn't. She expected each teacher to follow the suggested lesson plans that came with the curriculum. She expected each teammate to welcome the suggestions of others, even if they choose not to follow the advice. As Jane's expectations were not met, she felt betrayed and undermined. Unwilling to start a fight, she wanted out.

Pastor Carol responded to Jane, "Tell me a bit about the way your team leader performs. It's Sarah, correct?" Jane replied, "Sarah is no leader. Yes, she attends the meetings for the leaders of all the classes. Yes, she calls us together occasionally for a team meeting. However, that is about it. She is the total opposite of Charles when he was team leader. He micromanaged everything we did. He drove us nuts."

In both of these examples, Jane has personalized the problem. James and Sarah both failed her expectations. She is now angry with them personally, not upset with the overall dynamics of the team.

She has turned a team problem into a one-on-one problem with two different team members.

If, as suggested by the Dyers, team problems are viewed from the larger perspective of the norms the team has created and to which each member has agreed, it should be much easier to sort out disagreements. Personal expectations can be synchronized with the team's established norms. If they aren't in sync, the team needs to have a discussion until expectations become formalized as norms.

So, in this example, was there clarity within the team about the role of the team leader? If the leadership expectations were clear, was there a discussion about why the expectation was violated in this case? If yes, what came from that discussion? If no, why not? In the case of James, are there norms about how the curriculum is used? Are there norms about how one expresses and responds to criticism? When expectations become formally adopted norms, discussions will be about norms rather than devolving into personality clashes.

Pastor Carol continued, "It seems to me that the first thing that needs to happen in your group is a discussion about roles and expectations. I would be glad to facilitate such a conversation. However, I need to say, Jane, that it will produce some discomfort for everyone. I don't like conflict any more than you do. And if your team's discussion is honest, as it needs to be, it will generate some conflict. But in my experience, out of the short-term conflict will come clearer expectations of Sarah, the team leader, James, all of you who are teaching, and the team itself. You know, Jane, I have seen these types of conversations take place with incredibly good results. I am hoping and praying that you will trust your team members enough to be a part of the conversation. Once it is completed, you can make your own decision about whether you want to stay or leave the team. But, you know what? I am betting you will stay!"

us became editors and were given the authority to make final decisions on what was submitted; and several team members were designated to use their skills with software such as Excel and Power-
Point. When norms were violated, we created a policy that anyone
could name the violation, and we would have a team meeting to
resolve the issue. Finally, we agreed that disagreements were not to
be avoided; they were to be worked through. Because of our newly
created norms, we never reached a meltdown crisis again.

As the norms were created, our performance improved dramatically. Professors and fellow students commented on it. We became
very task oriented. When our work was done after eighteen intense
months, our team adjourned. We remain in touch with each other to
this day.

Tuckman's paradigm is very easy to remember. It is a great
teaching device as teams are set up in congregations. I find it extremely useful as a coach or team leader to say, "We are now engaged in classic storming behavior," or whichever other phase the
team is in. There is something about knowing that all healthy, creative teams go through these five phases that makes them more acceptable and tolerable. The fact that our team argued didn't mean
we were out of control. It meant we were in the storming phase.

In many ways, Tuckman's phases remind me of the grieving
phases developed by Elizabeth Kubler-Ross: denial, anger, bargain-
ing, depression, and acceptance.[2] A person who has experienced a
death can get stuck in the denial phase. It is healthy to experience
denial, unhealthy to get stuck in the denial phase of grieving. As a
congregational leader and manager of teams, what I need to be
concerned about is not a team that is storming. Storming is normal
team behavior. What I need to watch for is a team that gets stuck in
a phase such as storming. When stuck, I need to help teams understand the need to move beyond storming to norming.

How do we move from the storm to the norm? A coach, like our dean, helps us name the problems generating the storm. We then talk through possible solutions to the problems. Finally, we embrace one of the solutions. If it is something we will encounter again, the solution can be named a norm.

THE LENCIONI PARADIGM

Another way to analyze a team's behavior is to use Patrick Lencioni's now famous five dysfunctions of a team.[3] In his fabulous book, Lencioni tells a story in which a corporate management team is dysfunctional because of an absence of trust, fear of conflict, lack of commitment, avoidance of accountability, and inattention to results. As I will explain in the next chapter, I think these also happen to be the five dysfunctions of a congregation.

When our MBA team came together, we didn't know each other. As important, for better or worse, we knew that we had to work together for the next eighteen months. Therefore, in retrospect, it isn't surprising that we didn't trust each other enough to engage in healthy conflict over our team projects. Trust is earned. Only as our team worked, argued, and accomplished tasks together would we learn to trust each other.

It is easy to see how Lencioni's various dysfunctions flow in and out of each other, how interwoven with one another they are. Using my MBA team as an example, we feared conflict, which caused us to avoid holding one another accountable, which meant, ultimately, we didn't pay enough attention to the results (our lower grades). If teammates effectively hold each other accountable, they will inevitably come into conflict. If a team member isn't doing what needs to be done to get the desired results, someone has to hold the teammate accountable for poor work. Naming the obvious will produce some angry sparks.

Lack of commitment manifested itself in a couple of ways. In our team, one person clearly did not feel a need to produce results in a timely manner. But none of us were committed enough to the team's success to push performance issues that needed to be addressed. Yes, I complained about our lower grades but I didn't do what the dean did and ask, "What is the problem, and how do we solve it?"

In our team, the primary issue was fear of conflict. We tentatively liked each other and didn't want to rock our fragile relationships as a team. Unwittingly, by avoiding appropriate conflict over normal differences of opinion, we ensured that conflict would take place.

So each of Lencioni's five dysfunctions were present in our team. However, they were so interwoven with each other that it was hard to tell which of them was the presenting issue at any one point in time. As I have worked more with teams, I find this to be the norm. A team doesn't work through Lencioni's five dysfunctions the way a team moves through Tuckman's phases of team life. Lencioni's dysfunctions are swirling about within each of Tuckman's stages.

Putting Tuckman's and Lencioni's paradigms together, we gain powerful insights into team behavior and what is required to build a healthy team. Tuckman rightly sees the storming phase as crucial to the development of a team. Through a series of tough, conflict-inducing conversations, a team is able to create its own norms. Lencioni does a commendable job of describing the fear of conflict that, in effect, keeps many teams from ever explicitly naming the storming phase. Afraid of conflict, we avoid it. Attempting to avoid conflict, we create subliminal conflict that usually surfaces in unhelpful ways. Not getting through the storming phase, we don't create the norms needed to be effective. As a result, too many teams fail to move into the phase of effective performance.

In congregational teams, the fear of conflict is an omnipresent factor. However, conflict seems to be an unavoidable part of a faith journey. We see a lot of interpersonal conflict among the Hebrew people in their sojourn from slavery to freedom; read in the Gospels about conflict between Jesus and his disciples as well as between the disciples themselves; and study major conflicts in the church such as the establishment of the Nicene Creed or the Protestant Reformation. And yet, despite seeing the redemptive role such conflict has played in our faith traditions, we usually run from it in our congregations.

THE EXPECTATION MODEL

Most people do not come to church hoping or even expecting to engage in conflict. They want their family of faith to be a safe place where they don't have the hassles and criticism they face in the workplace and even in their families. However, many of us do not understand or believe that safe places are not necessarily conflict-free places.

A potential spin-off benefit of the use of teams is that congregational members can learn to disagree with members of their team. As members learn to process conflict in teams, is it reasonable to expect that they will do better at processing conflict in larger congregational settings? I think so. Healthy team behavior can be an incubator for healthy congregational behavior.

The Dyers maintain that the least helpful way of looking at intra-team conflict is to view it as the result of personality clashes.[4] Personalizing debates over issues leads to the conclusion that someone on the team has to either change their personality or leave the

However, what happens when a problem is, in fact, personality based? What does a team do when one member of the team exhibits behavior that is difficult? By "difficult" I mean personality traits such as argumentative, angry, or self-centered.

A disruptive personality is not necessarily a difficult personality, although we may perceive it that way. Many are the high-tech or scientific teams that have a very disruptive member who is crucial to the team's ultimate success. Gene Wade at UniversityNow, Jonathan Wolfson at Solazyme, and Jenny Fleiss and Jennifer Hyman, founders of Rent the Runway, were listed by *Forbes Magazine* among the "Twelve Most Disruptive Names in Business" in 2013. Being disruptive may have a bad name in congregations. Having disruptive ideas is a prized trait in many parts of the business and scientific worlds.[5]

Of course, there are people with disruptive ideas and others with disruptive personalities. Even the latter is not all bad. Steve Jobs and Adrianna Huffington are two individuals who are known to have some pretty disruptive, rough edges to their personalities. But their disruptive personalities are at the heart of their creativity. I'm not sure I would have enjoyed being on a team with them. But with them as members, I know my team would have been both innovative and highly productive. That being said, I wouldn't have relished being on a team with either Martin Luther or Paul of Tarsus! Talk about disruptive.

When I talk about a personality-based problem with a team member, the issue isn't the team member's disruptive ideas. It is their unwillingness to work with the team toward the identified goal. Their narcissism, anger, or passive aggressive behavior may destroy a team's internal cohesion. How do we resolve conflicts with such people? Obviously, the team leader can speak one-on-one with the "difficult person" to attempt to resolve the issue(s). In my experience, one-on-one conversations are the least effective.

In my book, *The Business of the Church*, I talk a bit about the ineffectiveness of annual performance reviews, which are basically one-on-one interactions between an employee and the boss. The reviews don't work because it is so easy for a low-performing staff member to dismiss what a boss says. The employee can walk away from the annual review thinking, "Well, the senior minister doesn't think I am doing a good job. But lots of people in the congregation tell me they like my work. I also think I am doing a good job. The boss is wrong. Just plain wrong."

One of the strengths of teams is they consist of multiple individuals. The team leader doesn't have to handle conflict by herself. The entire team can participate in the process. In good teams, the entire group confronts a problem, whether it be something that stands between the team and its goal, such as a lack of resources, or a difficult team member. For example, a team will talk with a member who shows disrespect for teammates by responding to constructive criticism with angry outbursts. When I was an associate pastor and the senior minister told me I had a problem, I could dismiss him as having bad judgment. When five teammates tell me I have a problem, it is almost impossible for me to dismiss them out of hand. After all, it isn't one person's opinion. It is a team opinion.

Let's revisit the sixth grade teaching team at St. Michael's Church. Jane and other members of the team have identified James as a problem. He isn't following the curriculum and doesn't prepare in advance to teach his classes. Worse, whenever anybody mentions these two realities to James, he gets angry. While Jane blames Sarah, the team leader, for not confronting James, isn't it the role of the team to have that kind of conversation? If the team has been appropriately trained and coached, the answer is yes. How might such a conversation between the team and James go?

Sarah: James, the other members of the team have asked me to call this meeting because they have some issues with the way you are performing as a team member.

James: Why didn't each of you speak to me directly? Why are you talking about me behind my back?

Jane: We don't want to talk about you behind your back, so we asked for this team meeting. We need to address this as a team rather than each of us having a one-on-one conversation with you about our concerns. Maybe the rest of us are doing something wrong that needs to be addressed in this conversation.

Michael: James, you have great strengths as a teacher. The students really love you; you come up with exciting ways to engage our kids with the Bible texts; and you are a committed Christian.

Jane: I agree. The issue isn't whether or not you are a good teacher or good person. The issue is that we have a curriculum. In order to use it, each of us on the team needs to prepare for our class in advance of Sunday morning. The curriculum allows for plenty of creativity, the type of creativity you bring to the classroom, in creating a lesson plan. But there is an expectation that each of us will prepare a lesson plan prior to entering the classroom.

James: You are giving me a pretty mixed message. On the one hand, you say I am a great teacher. On the other, you are suggesting that I am lazy or disorganized or both because I don't like to use prepared lesson plans. Make up your mind. Do you want a great teacher or an organized teacher?

Sarah: We want a great team. To me, we need to resolve a basic question: Do we want to make advance preparation of lesson plans an expectation for each team member? If not, what are our expectations regarding our team's teaching style and content?

After a lengthy discussion, everyone but James agreed that lesson plans were a basic expectation. They agreed to share their plans with each other so everyone knew what was happening in the classroom on those Sundays when they weren't present. James listened, clearly unhappy with the team's discussion. He finally said, "I can't be on this team. Each of you is a good teacher just as I think I am. But I just can't function with the expectations you have created for team members. I wish you well, but I need to find something else to do with my time."

The sixth grade teaching team went through a classic storming and norming conversation. The outcome of storming and norming is not always pleasant. Some team members may, like James, decide that the norms are inappropriate and leave. However, without the norms, the team will grow increasingly dysfunctional. Members will quit because of the team dysfunction, not because they disagree with the norms. Viewed from a larger perspective, James leaving the team over a disagreement regarding norms is better than him or others leaving the team because of growing interpersonal conflict. As a new team member is recruited to replace James, the new person needs to be informed, in advance, of the norms the team has created regarding lesson plans and other issues. If the person agrees to the norms, she or he can become a part of the team.

Part of having clear expectations in high-functioning teams is to establish well-defined roles for each team member. Who is doing what? When roles aren't clearly delineated, members will start stepping on each other's toes.

St. Mark Church has a team whose task is to ensure that all of the technical communication systems work on Sunday morning. This involves everything from microphones and speakers to large display screens and projectors for PowerPoint presentations. The team meets every Sunday before and after worship. The meeting before worship is to make sure that every person is clear about her or his responsibility. Who will set the volume on the voice amplification system? Who will make sure the images on the projection screen have the correct focus and sharpness? Who will be responsible if something breaks down during the service? As they leave their meeting, each person knows exactly what he or she is going to do. Roles are clarified. The likelihood of a successful product is high.

The team meets after worship as well. In the post-worship meeting, they reflect on any problems that have occurred and discuss any improvements they can make for the weeks ahead. They congratulate each other on especially good jobs. They discuss any unique work they will have for the following Sunday. Again, they leave clear about their job as a team and the role each person plays in making sure they are successful.

The worship technology team at St. Mark Church works well because roles are clear. By having brief organizational meetings, unnecessary conflict is eliminated. There may still be conflict, but it will be related to roles performed (or not) rather than personalities. Role clarification leads to definite expectations, which, in turn, reduces conflict.

But what about the team member who is just flat-out problematic time and again. Will we tolerate the intolerable in congregations? I have heard people say, "Well, Jesus told us that we need to forgive people seven times seventy times (that is, an infinite number of times)." Yes, he did say that. He also criticized disciples and non-disciples alike when they didn't meet expectations. Peter could testify to the fact that Jesus did not passively accept the unacceptable.

High-functioning teams understand and embrace accountability. When a team is entrusted with an important task in a congregation, it has a responsibility to get the job done. The group deals with anything that stands between the team and the accomplishment of its goal. It is irresponsible for a team not to reach its goal because it hasn't asked for enough resources. It is equally irresponsible for it to fail because team members refuse to hold each other accountable for their work.

In the business world, team members that fail get fired. Life in congregations, however, is different. At Western Church, we were having trouble with our ushering teams not functioning at appropriate level of effectiveness. Sometimes ushers simply didn't show up on their assigned Sunday. At other times, they wouldn't bother to escort visitors to a seat. The topic came up regularly at governing board meetings. One of our elders, a high-ranking military member, said, "If they aren't going to do the job right, then let's just fire them." There was a stunned silence until I broke out laughing. I responded, "Frank, we can't fire them. They are volunteers. They also happen to be contributors to the congregation in terms of time, energy, and money. This isn't the army. We can't just fire people."

Frank was never satisfied with that answer. He recognized that even though congregations are reluctant to fire volunteers or staff, we need to hold each other accountable in our congregational work. Susan Beaumont, a stellar congregational consultant, is one of the best writers I know on the subject of accountability. In a blog post, she writes:

> Many of us have learned to blindly accept less than desired or agreed upon outcomes. Often we choose to simply redo or complete a task ourselves, or work around a problem player. After all, congregations are volunteer organizations. What can you expect? We take what we can get.
>
> Each time that we fail to address a disappointing outcome with one volunteer, we send a harmful message to all of our volunteers. We communicate that the ministry itself isn't important enough to warrant excellence and accountability. We com-

municate that the overarching mission of the congregation is not
as important as the volunteer's feelings.[6]

When first reading Beaumont years ago, I thought she was being
a bit harsh on underperforming staff and volunteers. But when I
reflected on what happened when I didn't deal with such staff and
volunteers in my own ministry, I realized she is on the mark. By not
dealing with problematic behavior or performance, such conduct
gets worse. By not trying to hurt some individual's feelings, even
more feelings get hurt. Beaumont is absolutely correct when she
insists that accountability be made a part of congregational life and,
by my extension, team life. "Being harsh" and "holding people accountable to their agreements" are not synonymous terms.

Congregations should be able to hold people accountable in
ways consistent with their religious teachings. In a congregational
setting, it is appropriate to start a team with a discussion of the
theological underpinnings of accountability. Most of us believe that
God holds us accountable for the way we lead our lives. Moses
came down the mountain with what? He presented his people with
ten basic standards by which he and God would hold the people
accountable. Jesus repeatedly said that God holds us accountable for
what we do as well as how we do it. In the parable of the talents, for
example, each person is judged by what they did or did not do with
the talents entrusted to them.

As we establish a team, we can ask them, "How will you hold
one another accountable?" I have already discussed the norming
stage as crucial in this regard. In that phase, a team establishes its
norms and expectations. However, because humans are human,
those norms will be abused. So, what then?

Beaumont suggests that the more direct and specific we are in
dealing with problematic behavior by a team member, the more
likely we are to solve the problem. She writes about three very

concrete aspects of a situation that need to be addressed when having a discussion with someone exhibiting problematic behavior:

> *Situation*: Describe the situation. Be specific about when and where the behavior occurred, or was supposed to occur.
>
> *Behavior*: Describe the observable behavior. Don't use generalities and don't assume you know what the other person was thinking.
>
> *Impact*: Describe what you thought or felt in reaction to the behavior. [7]

It is a descriptive, rather than starkly accusatory, process. After laying out our perception of the issue, we can then ask, "Was all of this your intention?" This question allows the person to explain their perception of what happened or their reasons for doing what they did. The conversation can then move into a coaching mode with, "Well, if that was your intention, then you might try _____. I have found it to be successful." The final part of the conversation can return to the expectations to which the team has agreed with a renewed commitment to work toward the stated goals.

Congregations attract healthy and unhealthy people. So far, I have been discussing how a team can remedy problematic behavior by a reasonable, emotionally/mentally healthy person. What about dealing with an unreasonable, unhealthy person? As congregations, we feel called to care for the sick. How do we care for an individual whose emotional or mental unhealthiness produces behavior that negatively impacts the team's intrapersonal relationships? By unhealthy, I am not talking about someone who is a danger to others. Such people cannot serve on teams or elsewhere in a congregation, nor can individuals serve on teams when mental or emotional health problems are so significant that all attention must be devoted to caring for them. Please note that, for the purposes of this book, I am focusing on the individual's impact on the team ("all attention must be devoted to caring for them") rather than supplying a list of unhealthy behaviors.

Some teams make a decision to work around or accommodate a nondangerous, unhealthy person. This is certainly not the best strategy. The fact that a person is emotionally or mentally unhealthy does not mean, by itself, that he or she cannot be an effective team member, make valuable contributions, and be held accountable for her or his actions. In many instances, a conversation with this problematic person will produce positive results for the troubled team member and the team. A reminder of the collective goal can help turn an individual's attention to strategizing about how to work with the team, as well as providing assurance that the team will be supportive in those efforts.

As a pastor, I certainly understand why work-arounds happen. We don't want to exacerbate a person's problem by removing them from a team. Oftentimes, we aren't willing to confront them for fear of permanently alienating them from both the team and congregation. If everyone on a team agrees to a strategy of working with, rather than working around, an unhealthy team member, I am fine with it. (Most experts on teams would probably disagree with my assessment.) In this case, "working with" may involve a little "working around" in the sense that some team members may agree to carry slightly higher levels of work to lighten and focus the work of the unhealthy team member.

Such a strategy will reduce the efficiency of the team. But efficiency is not the only goal in a spiritual community. We are also called to include in our ministry individuals who are struggling in life. If attempts at conversation and accommodation are unsuccessful, and an unhealthy person continues to make it impossible for a team's work to be done, it will be necessary to ask the person to leave the team. Hopefully, a task can be found for them in the congregation where their unhealthy behavior does not damage the ministry or them.

CONCLUSION

The Dyers have a list of very specific behaviors that can undermine a team's culture and effectiveness. A good tool for analyzing how a team is functioning, their list includes not showing up for meetings; being late for meetings; not clearly demonstrating commitment to the work; not completing assignments in a timely manner (which causes everybody else to have to wait); competing for, rather than sharing, resources; not sharing credit for work well done; and not responding to emails, texts, or voice mail in a timely manner.

At first glance, these issues seem fairly minor. But having worked on teams, these are the errors team members make that get under my skin and are equally irritating to teammates when I act in this way. It is like a marriage, partnership, or any other relationship where individuals are working with each other in close quarters. It oftentimes isn't the egregious, big stuff that damages a relationship or team. It can be seemingly insignificant behavior.

In this chapter, I have discussed some of the most written about areas of team conflict. However, there are hundreds of other issues large and small to which one needs to attend. As we coach and participate in teams, reading about conflict is the best path I know to creating effective teams. Therefore, anyone committing to a team-driven congregation will need to read about handling such conflict. While there is much written on conflict, a simple Google search will provide you all the engaging reading you need. It is actually fun to see how teams are dealing with conflict in fields as different as the technology industry, the US military forces, and the nursing profession. Equally fascinating is finding the parallels between what people are doing in those fields and what we need to do in our congregations to build effective teams.

In the last chapter, I am going to apply some of our learnings regarding teams to the life of a congregation as a whole. As I have done research for this book while consulting with congregations, I have realized that everything that is true of a team is usually true of congregational life.

4

CONGREGATIONS AND CONCLUSIONS

At the same time I was researching for and writing this book, I began consulting with congregations around various issues. It quickly became clear to me that much of what I was learning about teams is directly applicable to the life of a congregation. Of course, congregations are definitely bigger than the seven members recommended for a team. Nonetheless, the knowledge about teams compiled in this book relates directly to our experiences in the life of a congregation.

THE FIVE DYSFUNCTIONS OF A CONGREGATION

Patrick Lencioni's five dysfunctions of a team match perfectly to five realities I have observed that create dysfunction in a congregation. As a consultant, I am often employed to lead strategic planning processes. However, the need for a strategic plan is typically rooted in some kind of dysfunction in the congregational life of my clients. As a result, I have become well versed in the five dysfunctions of a congregation.

ABSENCE OF TRUST

There is nothing more corrosive to the life of a congregation than an underlying absence of trust that may manifest itself as congregants not having confidence in their pastoral staff, the congregation's governing board, one another, or all three. Until trust is established within the congregation and with its leadership, the congregation will struggle to accomplish anything at all.

I always remind leaders in congregations that there is no reason congregants should trust them simply because they are leaders. Every day we read stories of leaders who have betrayed us. In business, government, the military forces, and, most relevant, religious communities, leaders have intentionally or unintentionally misled people who relied on them. In my lifetime, it started with Vietnam, when our leaders were less than forthright. Distrust morphed to a new level after Richard Nixon's Watergate fiasco. More specific to congregations, the number of religious leaders who have been exposed for sexual, financial, or other types of misconduct is staggering. Every week I read about another congregation that has had money stolen by a trusted employee or volunteer. When we regularly miss budget projections, have chronic staff issues, or fail to implement a strategic plan, we erode trust. Misconduct and incompetence within congregations have taken their toll on trust.

As a result, I do not condemn those who lack confidence in their congregational leaders. Rather, I implore the leaders to acknowledge the problem and then earn the allegiance of their congregants by behaving in trustworthy ways. Creating trust in a team or congregation must be at the top of every effective leader's list today. Without it, a congregation will never realize its calling.

A faith crisis begins when we start not to trust God. A congregational crisis begins when members question its leadership as trustworthy. Herein is the most fundamental congregational dysfunction.

Of course, all of this prompts the question, how do we build trust? Performance. It is a word many won't use in the church. When we make good on our promises, when we do what we say we are going to do, trust begins to grow like the proverbial mustard seed. When we act the way faithful people should, we build trust. Trust is results driven.

Crucially, we don't have to succeed at everything we attempt. But when we don't succeed, we have to acknowledge it. Think what you will about Ronald Reagan's politics. He was a great leader. At the heart of his leadership style was a willingness to own mistakes. So often, I would turn on the television while President Reagan was saying, "As Harry Truman said, 'the buck stops here.' I take full responsibility for this failure." Since the American people are fundamentally a forgiving people, we forgave the president. Perhaps we forgave too readily and should have demanded better answers about why there wouldn't be another failure.

But the key point for this discussion is that people develop trust in leaders who do what they say they will do and then acknowledge problems that inevitably develop when events don't unfold as planned. People do not trust leaders who promise something but don't deliver it. If a congregation's leaders say they are going to grow the congregation, they had better (1) grow the congregation or (2) acknowledge why it hasn't grown. If a budget is supposed to be balanced, it better be balanced, or there must be sound answers why it ended up in a deficit.

FEAR OF CONFLICT

Earlier in this book, I described the way my MBA team struggled at first because we didn't want to offend each other by being critical of another team member's work. In like manner, fear of conflict routinely inhibits the work of a congregation. We want to be friends with everyone in our congregations. However, we have come to equate being unfriendly with being in conflict.

Now I know that some of my readers are saying, "Fear of conflict? I don't see any such fear in my congregation. We are constantly arguing with each other." Indeed, there is much unhealthy strife in congregations; however, I contend that the unhealthy conflict flows equally from a fear of conflict and conflict itself. Let me give you an example.

A congregation I knew well had been in existence for over 130 years. Upon her arrival, the new pastor, Jane, studied the congregation's history but found no evidence of any significant conflict. The one exception involved Jane's predecessor. The conflict around him was dreadful. He refused to ordain women as ruling elders even though the congregation kept electing women to that position. Because the pastor wouldn't officiate, the local judicatory had to come in and conduct the ordinations and installations of the female officers. A huge battle ensued between the majority of congregants who wanted women elders and a small minority of members who supported the pastor. Ultimately, he left the congregation, realizing that his theology was not compatible with the beliefs of the majority of the congregation.

On the first Sunday after Jane arrived, she heard the elders talking as they planned to serve Communion. One elder said, "I will serve the front-left part of the sanctuary, because if I serve the front-right side, James won't take Communion from me. He is one of the supporters of the former pastor, and I was not." Jane was stunned. How could this argument have escalated to the point where Christians wouldn't receive Communion from one another?

In fact, the issue at the church Jane served had never been the ordination of women. The problem was the 130 years of congregational history that preceded the battle over female ruling elders.

Despite going through civil wars and world wars, Great Depressions and the Gilded Age, debates over evolution and Christology, the congregation never had a significant argument. There is only one way to explain such a lack of conflict—a fear of it. For more than a century, this particular congregation had been suppressing disagreement over any one of hundreds of perfectly legitimate issues. When all of the suppressed anger came spewing forth during the debate over ordaining women elders, it produced a very nasty, traumatic battle.

From a systems theory perspective, it was predictable that once Jane arrived, the waters calmed. The system reverted to its conflict-averse style. Once she figured out what was happening, Jane started preaching, teaching, and counseling the members about the need for healthy conflict.

Moses argued with his people in the desert. Jesus argued with his disciples. Paul argued with the members of congregations he started. Great leaders are not afraid of conflict. They don't enjoy it. But they understand the positive role a good argument can play in getting to the Promised Land.

There is nothing wrong with conflict in a congregation as long as the style of argument is constructive rather than destructive, issue oriented rather than personality oriented, and looking to the future rather than debating what could have or should have happened in the past. Teams that learn to argue together are highly effective. The same is true of congregations as a whole.

LACK OF COMMITMENT

Members of teams rightly get very irritated with teammates who demonstrate a lack of commitment. The same is true of congregational members. I can't count the many times I have heard a mem-

ber say, "John, I am tired of doing all the work. Get someone else to
do it. Recruit some of the people who benefit from our ministry but
do nothing." It is a common, reasonable refrain heard in most congregations.

Of course, sometimes the people complaining about doing all the
work have no real desire to mobilize the rest of the members. They
perform all the work because it allows them to control everything.
But in most instances, the complaints ring true. Too many congregants don't feel committed to the work of the congregation.

A key part of congregational leadership is finding ways to engage members. In this book, I have contended that one way to
increase commitment is to use teams. As people serve on teams
doing something discrete, they develop a sense of ownership and
commitment to the overall ministry as well. A commitment to the
micro transforms into a commitment to the macro. But regardless of
how one does it, creating a widespread sense of commitment to the
success of the congregation is a key leadership function.

What are other ways to create commitment to a congregation's
ministry? It is a broad topic outside the scope of this book. However, let me mention a few things. As a consultant and previously as a
pastor, I have found that a carefully crafted strategic planning process creates a sense of commitment and ownership if there are highly visible signs of the plan's implementation. Small groups focusing
on personal spiritual growth or mission projects can generate pro-
found commitment to the small group and, by extension, the larger
ministry. Stewardship campaigns must develop a sense of commitment to succeed. As a pastor, I found personal testimonies to be the
most compelling way to allow members to express their commitment and why they give. This, in turn, causes other members to
examine why they do or do not support a ministry generously with
their time, talents, and money. The list goes on. However, one thing
I know. If there is a lack of commitment within a congregation or

one group of members thinks they are carrying the bulk of the responsibility for a congregation's life, it will lead to dispirited congregational life.

AVOIDANCE OF ACCOUNTABILITY

When teammates in a commercial corporation don't hold one another accountable for work results, the work rarely gets done in a timely, efficient, or effective manner. The same is true in a congregation. Pastors, governing boards, and teams routinely are not held accountable for what they do or don't do. Yes, there are annual performance reviews for staff. But if the staff continues to underperform the next year, are there any consequences for the employees? Not usually. Why? We seem to think that our religious traditions are more about forgiveness than accountability when, in fact, they are about both. We need forgiveness because we haven't done that which we were supposed to do.

Another factor working against creating a culture of accountability is, once again, fear of conflict. As the head of staff, I might feel an associate pastor isn't doing his job. The first thing I have to do is get over my fear that my colleague will dislike me for saying, "I may be wrong, but it doesn't feel like you are getting your assignment done." It is the same with laypeople. Will they quit the church if they are held accountable for not doing something they said they would do? Accountability is feared not just because people don't like being judged. Most don't like being the judge.

Our theology can help us build a culture of accountability. Every major religion teaches that we should be responsible. Irresponsibility betrays a core value of our faith traditions. As we work on building healthy congregational cultures, we need to align our organizational behavior with our theology. If we know we will be held

accountable (in a loving, caring manner) for the outcomes of our
efforts, most of us are more likely to produce positive outcomes.
Not holding each other responsible sends a very bad message. We
basically tell each other, "I don't really care what you do. Do it
right. Do it wrong. I'm not going to say anything one way or the
other."

INATTENTION TO RESULTS

Inattention to results is a piece of the accountability issue. When
interviewing with a congregation to be a strategic planning consultant, the first task I have is to convince them that the plan will make
a difference. For many, prior efforts at strategic planning have left a
bad taste in their mouths. They poured much time, prayer, and energy into a planning process at work, in a community organization, or
their congregation from which absolutely nothing came. However,
the plan was never implemented. "Why bother again?" people ask
me. "How can you assure us that something will happen this time
around?"

At Western Church, our planning processes became much more
productive when we began creating a performance measure for each
and every strategy. Every January, the congregation's governing
board asked those assigned a strategy to report their progress. The
leaders never beat up a staff person, team, or committee that didn't
hit their performance measures, but they held themselves and the
people assigned the task accountable. By asking the implementers to
reflect on the performance measure they set for themselves, the
governing body says, "Your work matters. We are committed to
results."

In management circles, there is an old axiom that goes, "You
can't manage what you can't measure." Our inattention to results is

oftentimes the consequence of never defining an intended outcome. What is our intended result in establishing a Sunday school for children? There are many ways to answer that question. Whatever the reply, measurements need to be created that allow everyone involved in the program to determine whether or not the intended results are occurring. The same is true for each and every program in a congregation.

OTHER TEAM INSIGHTS THAT ILLUMINATE CONGREGATIONAL LIFE

Starting Just about Anything

As I studied the research and literature on teams, I realized that, in my ministry, I had been entirely too relaxed in the ways I started programs, teams, committees, or just about anything else. As we have learned, starting a team requires great intentionality. There needs to be a clear purpose, members of the team need to be chosen carefully, team size has to be determined, and ongoing team coaching provided as needed. While I did some of that with various start-ups at Western Church, I didn't do it with the discipline required. As I have learned in my consulting work, I am not alone in my failures to be more systematic when getting things started on the right foot.

A good idea is just that, nothing more. Once a good idea reaches the leadership of a congregation, it needs to be evaluated carefully. The initial filter through which all good concepts must flow is the congregation's primary purpose. Does the idea match what the congregation wants to do? If there isn't a clear connection between the proposal and the congregation's larger strategic purpose, which has hopefully been laid out in a plan, then it needs to be set aside. If the idea furthers the primary purpose of the congregation, the next question becomes, what will it take to implement it? How much money, staff time, volunteer effort, and building space will it require?

Just as we shouldn't start teams unless we are prepared to do it correctly, we shouldn't begin programs in our congregations unless we have considered everything that will lead to the success of a program. In start-ups, key questions include: What type of structure does the program need—a team, committee, staff? What are the skill sets required for the people managing and implementing it? Who in the congregation's leadership will provide ongoing supervision or coaching? What resources does it require? Do we have them or can we acquire them? When these questions are addressed before initiating a program, the likelihood of the effort succeeding increases exponentially.

Leaving Silos Behind

One reason businesses turn to teams is that teamwork breaks through the "silo system." For example, in a twentieth-century company, it wasn't unusual for research and development to design a product, manufacturing to make the product, marketing to sell the product, and finance to estimate its profitability. In twenty-first-century, team-driven companies, a single team will do most, if not all, of those functions. For example, a team at Apple will come up with a new product, consider the manufacturing and marketing issues involved, and think through projected profit margins. The team does everything except make the product. In this type of team environment, people are not allowed to work in compartments isolated from one another. Everyone interacts with each other. Team-driven organizations have discovered that this model produces ongoing synergies and efficiencies that the old model of silos could not realize.

To make the major points in his book on teams, Patrick Lencioni tells a parable about team building. [1] It involves a classic twentieth-century-style company in which the management team consists of the usual cast—a chief executive officer (CEO) and chief operating officer, as well as the heads of the marketing, finance, and research and development departments. When a new CEO arrives, she attempts to mold them into a team. Her biggest challenge is to break down the "this is my area of responsibility" mentality. She wants to replace that approach with "making this company profitable is the responsibility of all of us." In other words, she wants to move from a segmented to systemic approach.

As a consultant, I experience the silo approach in congregation after congregation. The music people will say, "We produce inspiring music Sunday after Sunday. We aren't the reason attendance is declining." Maybe not, but is such a "I did my job, and that is the end of my responsibility" attitude helpful? No, because it reflects a silo approach to ministry. I have seen booming Christian education departments, fabulous mission committees, and caring membership committees assume the same attitude. They know the congregation as a whole is struggling. But they continue to assert that they aren't the problem.

The larger a congregation becomes, the more likely it is to adopt a silo approach in its staff design and performance expectations. They hire a music person to work with the music ministry. No one explains to the music person that the goal is a successful ministry, not just a successful music ministry.

If one believes in congregational systems theory as I do, no one can adopt the silo approach to diagnosing the strengths and weaknesses of a congregation. In the life of a congregation, everything is so interwoven and connected that it is impossible to create neat segments. Whether or not the facilities are clean and safe is as important for Christian education as it is for music people. If the congregation isn't growing, where will the new students come for Christian education classes or new choir members to replace those who leave? No one should be able to claim that they have succeeded at their job if the greater body (the congregation) is not doing well.

We move out of silos when we create a sense of team among the key staff as well as within the governing board. When members of congregational staffs and governing boards stop representing the interests that are nearest and dearest to their hearts but start advancing the good of the entire congregation, the body is on the way to health and holiness. It is magical to behold when it happens.

CONCLUSION

I started this book by saying that younger generations aren't keen about serving on committees but are energized at the possibility of doing God's work in teams. It is also a consensus among those who study generational differences that today's younger generations are less interested in governance than in doing work that has a tangible, measureable outcome. So when we try to engage and mobilize our members by offering them opportunities to govern or work on a committee, we are facing an uphill journey.

To engage our members, we need to give them chances to practice the most basic and simple mandates of our faith—feeding the hungry, visiting the sick, or standing up for justice. These are the activities younger generations have been doing since they were in high school. Most educational institutions require students to do a set number of hours of volunteer work in the community. The younger generations have learned just how exciting it is to feed a homeless person, care for an aging senior in a retirement home, clean up trash on a river's edge, or help out in an animal rescue shelter. These tasks are clear; the directions about what to do are specific; we know when we are finished because we can see the finished product—a fed person, cared for senior, cleaned up river's edge, or safe animal.

If we are to mobilize people to do God's work in congregational settings, using the team model is a no-brainer. However, teams need to be given the same kind of meaningful work people experience in the types of activities I just described. The days of people feeling satisfied with church busywork or even congregational governance are over. The days of mobilizing members for church mission work are upon us.

As a consultant, I see congregation after congregation trying to engage its members as well as those "spiritual but not religious" folks outside their doors. In my experience, a basic step toward engaging them is an invitation to serve on a team. By working together with people who share their commitment to a very specific task, individuals will become engaged not just with their teammates but with God. They will also quickly feel ownership in the congregation that creates team opportunities.

It is my hope and prayer that this book has helped readers see the opportunities teams represent for congregational life as well as some of the specific steps we need to take when establishing them. May God be with us all as we work to mobilize our members to build a just, peaceful, and spiritually grounded world.

NOTES

INTRODUCTION

1. Patrick Lencioni, *The Five Dysfunctions of a Team: A Leadership Fable* (San Francisco: Jossey-Bass, 2002).

1. TEAMS AND COMMITTEES

1. *Compact Edition of the Oxford English Dictionary*, vol. 1 (Glasgow: Oxford University Press, 1971).

2. Ibid.

3. Dan Hotchkiss, *Governance and Ministry: Rethinking Board Leadership* (Herndon, VA: Alban Institute, 2009), 59.

4. Hotchkiss, 75.

5. Eilene Zimmerman, "Working Relationships Across Generations," *New York Times*, September 24, 2011, www.nytimes.com/2011/09/25/jobs/25career.html?_r=0.

6. Daniel H. Pink, *Drive: The Surprising Truth About What Motivates Us* (New York: Riverhead Books, 2009), 91.

7. Army News Service, "Why Soldiers Fight," May 15, 2014, usmilitary.about.com/cs/army/a/soldiersfight.htm.

8. Pink, 94.

9. Westminster Shorter Catechism Question 1, accessed December 7, 2014, www.shortercatechism.com/resources/wsc/wsc_001.html.

10. Emily Esfahani Smith and Jennifer Aaker, "Millennial Searchers," *New York Times*, December 1, 2013, Sunday Review Section, 1.

11. Ibid.

2. STARTING TEAMS

1. Brian X. Chen, "Simplifying the Bull: How Picasso Helps to Teach Apple's Style—Inside Apple's Internal Training Program," *New York Times*, August 10, 2014, www.nytimes.com/2014/08/11/technology/-inside-apples-internal-training-program-.html?module=Search&mab Reward=relbias%3As%2C%7B%221%22%3A%22RI%3A9%22%7 D&_r=0.

2. Edwin Friedman, *Generation to Generation: Family Process in Church and Synagogue* (New York: Guilford Press, 1985).

3. William G. Dyer, W. Gibb Dyer, Jr., and Jeffrey H. Dyer, *Team Building,* 4th ed. (San Francisco: Jossey-Bass, 2007), 21.

4. J. Richard Hackman, *Leading Teams* (Boston: Harvard Business School Press, 2002), 62.

5. Ibid., 75.

6. Ibid., 73.

7. Ibid., 83.

8. Adam Bryan, "Jennifer Dulski of Change.org, on Problem-Solving," *New York Times*, December 1, 2013 Business Section, 2.

9. Dyer, Dyer, and Dyer, 30.

10. Hackman, 122.

11. National Oceanographic and Atmospheric Association Office of Diversity, "Tips to Improve Interaction among the Generations: Traditionalists, Boomers, X'ers and Nexters," accessed December 1, 2014, www.biz.colostate.edu/mti/tips/pages/interactionamongthegenerations.aspx.

12. Dyer, Dyer, and Dyer, 32.

13. Ivan Steiner, "What Project Team Size Is Best," accessed December 1, 2014, www.articlesnatch.com/Article/What-Project-Team-Size-Is-Best-/589717#.VH34zTHF98E.

14. Dan Hotchkiss, *Governance and Ministry: Rethinking Board Leadership* (Herndon, VA: Alban Institute, 2009).

15. Lynda Gratton and Tamara J. Erickson, "Eight Ways to Build Collaborative Teams." *Harvard Business Review on Building Better Teams.* (Boston: Harvard Business Review Press, 2011), 45–72.

16. Ibid., 65.

17. Gregory E. Huszczo, *Tools for Team Leadership* (Boston: Davies-Black, 2010), 7.

18. Ibid., 4.

19. Hackman, 225.

20. Huszczo, 11.

21. Tim Carman, "Rose's Luxury Chef Aaron Silverman Masters the Art of Serious Play," *Washington Post*, August 26, 2014, www.washingtonpost.com/lifestyle/food/roses-luxury-chef-aaron-silverman-masters-the-art-of-serious-play/2014/08/25/dfc0d674-274d-11e4-8593-da634b334390_story.html?hpid=z1.

3. CREATING A HEALTHY TEAM

1. Bruce Tuckman, "Developmental Sequences in Small Groups," *Psychology Bulletin* 65 (1965): 384–99.

2. Elisabeth Kübler-Ross, *On Death and Dying* (New York: MacMillan, 1969).

3. Patrick Lencioni, *The Five Dysfunctions of a Team* (San Francisco: Jossey-Bass, 2002).

4. William G. Dyer, W. Gibb Dyer, Jr., and Jeffrey H. Dyer, *Team Building,* 4th ed. (San Francisco: Jossey-Bass, 2007), 117.

5. Caroline Howard, "The 12 Most Disruptive Names In Business: The Full List," *Forbes Magazine*, March 27, 2013, www.forbes.com/sites/

carolinehoward/2013/03/27/the-12-most-disruptive-names-in-business-the-full-list/.

    6. Susan Beaumont, "You Disappointed Me," Congregational Consulting Group website, accessed December 1, 2014, www.congregationalconsulting.org/you-disappointed-me/?utm_source=Subscribers&utm_campaign=0610defc3f-Perspectives_XIV_Beaumont_09_22_2014&utm_medium=email&utm_term=0_e863323d31-0610defc3f-156311457&ct=t(Perspectives_XV)&mc_cid=0610defc3f&mc_eid=d26f6cb438.

    7. Ibid.

4. CONGREGATIONS AND CONCLUSIONS

    1. Patrick Lencioni, *The Five Dysfunctions of a Team: A Leadership Fable* (San Francisco: Jossey-Bass, 2002).

BIBLIOGRAPHY

Army News Service. "Why Soldiers Fight." May 15, 2014. usmilitary.about.com/cs/army/a/soldiersfight.htm.

Beaumont, Susan. "You Disappointed Me." Congregational Consulting Group website. Accessed December 1, 2014. www.congregationalconsulting.org/you-disappointed-me/?utm_source=Subscribers&utm_campaign=0610defc3f-Perspectives_XIV_Beaumont_09_22_2014&utm_medium=email&utm_term=0_e863323d31-0610defc3f-156311457&ct=t(Perspectives_XV)&mc_cid=0610defc3f&mc_eid=d26f6cb438.

Bryan, Adam. "Jennifer Dulski of Change.org, on Problem-Solving." *New York Times*. December 1, 2013. Business Section.

Carman, Tim. "Rose's Luxury Chef Aaron Silverman Masters the Art of Serious Play." *Washington Post*. August 26, 2014. www.washingtonpost.com/lifestyle/food/roses-luxury-chef-aaron-silverman-masters-the-art-of-serious-play/2014/08/25/dfc0d674-274d-11e4-8593-da634b334390_story.html?hpid=z1.

Chen, Brian X. "Simplifying the Bull: How Picasso Helps to Teach Apple's Style—Inside Apple's Internal Training Program." *New York Times*. August 10, 2014. www.nytimes.com/2014/08/11/technology/-inside-apples-internal-training-program-.html?module=Search&mabReward=relbias%3As%2C%7B%221%22%3A%22RI%3A9%22%7D&_r=0.

Compact Edition of the Oxford English Dictionary. Vol. 1. Glasgow: Oxford University Press, 1971.

Dyer, William G., W. Gibb Dyer, Jr., and Jeffrey H. Dyer. *Team Building*. 4th ed. San Francisco: Jossey-Bass, 2007.

Friedman, Edwin. *Generation to Generation: Family Process in Church and Synagogue*. New York: Guilford Press, 1985.

Gratton, Lynda, and Tamara J. Erickson. *Harvard Business Review on Building Better Teams*. Boston: Harvard Business Review Press, 2011.

Hackman, J. Richard. *Leading Teams*. Boston: Harvard Business School Press, 2002.

Hotchkiss, Dan. *Governance and Ministry: Rethinking Board Leadership.* Herndon, VA: Alban Institute, 2009.

Howard, Caroline. "The 12 Most Disruptive Names In Business: The Full List." *Forbes Magazine.* March 27, 2013. www.forbes.com/sites/carolinehoward/2013/03/27/the-12-most-disruptive-names-in-business-the-full-list/.

Huszczo, Gregory E. *Tools for Team Leadership.* Boston: Davies-Black, 2010.

Kübler-Ross, Elisabeth. *On Death and Dying.* New York: MacMillan, 1969.

Lencioni, Patrick. *The Five Dysfunctions of a Team: A Leadership Fable.* San Francisco: Jossey-Bass, 2002.

National Oceanographic and Atmospheric Association Office of Diversity. "Tips to Improve Interaction among the Generations: Traditionalists, Boomers, X'ers and Nexters." Accessed December 1, 2014. www.biz.colostate.edu/mti/tips/pages/interactionamongthegenerations.aspx.

Pink, Daniel H. *Drive: The Surprising Truth About What Motivates Us.* New York: Riverhead Books, 2009.

Smith, Emily Esfahani, and Jennifer Aaker. "Millennial Searchers." *New York Times.* December 1, 2013. Sunday Review Section.

Steiner, Ivan. "What Project Team Size Is Best." Accessed December 1, 2014. www.articlesnatch.com/Article/What-Project-Team-Size-Is-Best-/589717#.VH34zTHF98E.

Tuckman, Bruce. "Developmental Sequences in Small Groups." *Psychology Bulletin* 65 (1965): 384–99.

Westminster Shorter Catechism Question 1. Accessed December 7, 2014. www.shortercatechism.com/resources/wsc/wsc_001.html.

Zimmerman, Eilene. "Working Relationships Across Generations." *New York Times.* September 24, 2011. www.nytimes.com/2011/09/25/jobs/25career.html?_r=0.